B

BEYOND VEIL AND HOLY WAR

Islamic Teachings and Muslim Practices with Biblical Comparisons

Saleem Ahmed, Ph.D.

*Moving Pen Publishers, Inc.,
Honolulu, Hawaii, USA*

BEYOND VEIL AND HOLY WAR:
Islamic Teachings and Muslim Practices
with Biblical Comparisons

ISBN 0-9717655-0-2

Published by

Moving Pen Publishers, Inc.
P.O. Box 25155, Honolulu, HI 96825, USA

www.BeyondVeilAndHolyWar.com

Copy-editing: Reynold Feldman, Ph.D.
(reynold22@hawaii.rr.com)

Publication consultant: Welmon "Rusty" Walker, President
That New Publishing Company, Honolulu.
www.ThatNewPublishingCompany.com

Manufactured in the USA

1 2 3 4 5 6 7 8 9 10

This book is dedicated to
all the innocent lives that have been lost
senselessly and tragically at the hands of
terrorism–whether State-sponsored or
inspired by zealots. May humanity
be guided onto the Right Path.

TABLE OF CONTENTS

PART I. THE CURRENT SITUATION

PART II. A VISION OF THE FUTURE

SOME REFLECTION POINTS FOR MUSLIMS

THE TEACHING

The Muslim holy book, the Qur'an, reminds us that "God sent prophets to all nations of the world" (Qur'an 10:47); that we are to "respect all equally—even those unnamed" (4:152); and that "the name of God is commemorated in monasteries, churches, synagogues, and mosques" (22:40). Thus, shouldn't Muslims respect, as messengers of God, founders of all religions who asked people to believe in one Supreme God and lead a righteous life? Shouldn't we unite around God's Message rather than divide because of messengers?

The Qur'an also urges Muslims to "invite (all) to the Way of your Lord with wisdom and beautiful preaching; and discuss with them in ways that are best and most gracious" (Qur'an 16:125). Thus, shouldn't we extend friendship to others rather than denigrate them?

THE PRACTICE

Prophet Muhammad* declared, "Whoever revives a *Sunnah* (see Glossary) which dies after me will be rewarded in the Hereafter; and whoever introduces some evil innovation which was not approved by God or His messenger will be punished" (Tirmidhi 168). Thus, shouldn't we consider those purported sayings and actions of the prophet, which appear to contradict the Qur'an, as possible innovations? (Note: The asterisk stands for "peace be upon him".)

The prophet* also declared, "Avoid inflicting the prescribed penalties on Muslims as much as you can and if there is a way out, let a man go. For it is better for a leader to make a mistake in forgiving than a mistake in punishing" (Tirmidhi 3570). Thus, shouldn't we show compassion for human weaknesses rather than trying to out-do each other in exceeding even the harshest punishment found in the Qur'an or Hadeeth for any particular sin?

GLOSSARY

*	As a mark of respect, the asterisk after a prophet's name will mean "peace be upon him."
☛	Notation used in this book to draw readers' attention to calls for Ijtihad, or soul-searching (see "Ijtihad" below).
Abu Bakar	The first Caliph after Muhammad* died.
Adhan	The Muslim call to prayer (salat).
Aisha	One of Muhammad's* 13 wives. Except for Aisha, all other wives were either divorcees or widows whom he* married to provide support and protection.
Ali	The fourth Caliph after Muhammad*. Shia Muslims claim he should have been the first Caliph.
Asr	Late afternoon obligatory prayer.
Ayah	An individual verse in the Qur'an. Plural: Ayat.
A.D.	Anno Domini. Used to indicate that a time division falls within the Christian era. This is now being replaced by C.E. (see below).
A.H.	Anno Hijri. Used to indicate that a time division falls within the Muslim era. A.H. marks the beginning of the Muslim calendar, starting from 622 C.E.
B.C.E.	Before the Common (or Christian) Era. Refers to the time period before Jesus Christ was born.
Bismillah	"In the name of Allah (God)." Muslim invocation.
Caliph	(Khalifa in Arabic). Successor of Muhammad* as the temporal and spiritual leader of Muslims.
C.E.	Common, or Christian, era. Used to indicate a time division that falls within the period after Christ's birth.
Dinar	Unit of currency.
Dirham	Unit of currency.
Fajr	The obligatory morning prayer, before sunrise.
Fard	Something which is obligatory for Muslims. It also

	refers to the obligatory part of prayers.
Fatwa	Legal opinion concerning Muslim Law.
Gabriel	The arch-angel who conveyed God's Message to Muhammad*.
Gemara	A commentary on the Mishnah, forming the second part of the Talmud.
Hadeeth	Sayings and examples of Muhammad*. While the plural is Ahadeeth, we will use Hadeeth for both singular and plural. (Alternate spelling: Hadith).
Halal	Anything lawful and permitted in Islam.
Haj	Pilgrimage to Mecca, obligatory on all Muslims if they can do so physically and financially.
Haraam	Anything unlawful or prohibited in Islam.
Haram	Sacred.
Hijrah	Migration of Muhammad* from Mecca to Medina in 622 C.E., at the invitation of the leaders of Medina. This marks the beginning of the Muslim calendar.
Hoor	"Companions with big eyes" in Paradise. Also: houri.
Ijtihad	A call for introspection and soul-searching, preferably collectively, by Muslims to seek answers to complex issues confronting them. Traditionally performed by "competent" people, my call is for all Muslims to participate in this matter of utmost importance.
Imam	Leader of the congregational prayer (salat); also used to refer to a religious leader.
Isha	The obligatory prayer at night.
Isnad	The chain of transmitters of any Hadeeth.
Injeel	The revelations that were sent down during the time of prophet Isa* (Jesus); the New Testament.
Jalbab	A long, loose fitting outer garment worn by Arabs.
Jihad	To strive for righteousness and to control the base self. Examples include helping eradicate injustice, oppression, and misinformation, and helping spread knowledge. It also includes self-improvement efforts such as dieting, trying to give up smoking, and fighting low self-esteem. And it also includes defensive war

	against religious discrimination.
Jinn	Beings "made from fire free of smoke" (Qur'an 55:15). They co-inhabit the universe with us.
Ka'bah	The first house of worship on earth for the One God. Tradition holds that it was originally built by Adam* and reconstructed by Abraham* and his elder son Ismail*. It is in Mecca, and all Muslims around the world face it during their daily prayers.
Kafir	A disbeliever in One God.
Khadijah	Muhammad's* first wife. She was about 20 years older than Muhammad* and had had two previous marriages.
Khalifah	Caliph; successor of the prophet.
Koran	The Qur'an; considered an incorrect transliteration.
Maghrib	The obligatory prayer performed at sunset.
Masjid	The Muslim house of worship; mosque.
Matan	The substance/text of a Hadeeth.
Mishnah	(or Mishna) The collection of Jewish traditions compiled about A.D. 200 and made the basic part of the Talmud.
Muhajir	A person who does hijrah (migration); a refugee.
Mujahid	A person who does jihad; plural, mujahiddin.
Mut'a	Temporary marriage.
Pbuh	"Peace be upon him." A common phrase added by Muslims whenever they mention the name of Muhammad* or other prophets. Pbuh is replaced by the asterisk (*) in this book.
Qiblah	The direction that Muslims face while offering prayers.
Qur'an	The Muslim holy book. Qur'an means "recitation."
Rajam	Stoning adulterers to death.
Ramadan	The month of fasting for Muslims.
Rasulullah	Messenger of Allah (God). Also: Rasool-Allah.
Rtd.	Abbreviation for "retired".
Sabians	Ancient monotheistic people probably living in the Middle East. Not much is known about them. See Abdullah Yusuf Ali's note No. 76 (Ali 1989)

Sahabi	Companion of the prophet (plural, sahaba).
Sahih	Authentic. This term also refers to some Hadeeth compilations, such as those of Bukhari and Muslim.
Salat	The five daily obligatory prayers for Muslims.
Shahadah	Declaration of faith. When converting to Islam, a person declares: "I believe in God, His angels, His prophets, His books, and the Day of Judgment." Another shahadah is: "I testify there is no deity but God and that Muhammad* is His prophet."
Shaheed	A martyr. Someone who dies in the cause of God.
Shariah	Islamic law. Included in this book under Hadeeth.
Shia	One of the two major Muslim sects. Followers are called Shias or Shiites. The other major sect is Sunni.
Shura	Consultation.
Sunnah	Examples of the prophet's* actions. These are included here under Hadeeth (the prophet's* sayings).
Sunni	One of the two major Muslim sects. Followers are called Sunnis. The other major sect is Shia.
Surah	A chapter in the Qur'an.
Talmud	The authoritative body of Jewish tradition comprising the Mishnah and Gemara.
Torah	The Revelation that God sent down to Moses*; the first five books of the Hebrew Scriptures/Old Testament.
Ulema	People knowledgeable about Islam.
Umar	The second Caliph after Muhammad*.
Ummah	Global community of Muslims.
Umm Salma	One of Muhammad's* wives.
Uthman	The third Caliph after Muhammad*.
Wudu	Purification (ablution) performed before praying or reading the Qur'an.
Zakah	The obligatory tax on Muslims, used for charitable purposes. It is considered an act of worship. Also: any righteous act for purification of one's self.
Zina	Illegal sexual intercourse.
Zuhr	The obligatory prayer, shortly after noon.

INTRODUCTION
Why this Book?

Many months have passed since the September 11th tragedy. The world, not yet fully recovered from the premeditated and cold-blooded murder of thousands, is groping for answers. How, people ask, can any religion incite its followers to such cruel acts? Islam stands accused. After all, impressions of this religion among non-Muslims are stained by reports of suicide attacks, hijacking, hostage taking, holy war ("jihad"), and terrorism–exacerbated by stories of veiled women ("hijab"), four wives, three pronouncements for divorce, and accounts of destroying statues and prohibiting religious freedom. Thus, the average non-Muslim perhaps cannot help but wonder how any sane person (especially a woman) can follow this faith. The fact that many Muslim countries reportedly have corrupt leaders, are embroiled in sectarian Shia-Sunni infighting, and have rampant poverty only increases the confusion leading many non-Muslims to look upon Islam as a "socio-cultural pollutant" and a "religio-political threat."

I have been working on this manuscript for more than eight years now and was hoping to review it further. However, the post-September 11th desire among non-Muslims to understand whether such horrendous acts really can be based upon Islamic teachings necessitated that I publish my thoughts post-haste. Thus, what follows should still be considered "initial thoughts," subject to refinement. Feedback from readers will be appreciated highly.

The inspiration to put these thoughts together in the present form came from several students who have attended my lectures in Hawaii on Islam over the past several years. They have come to regard Islam as a broad-minded, progressive religion, one that can offer spiritual satisfaction and intellectual fulfillment to many. I thank them for encouraging me to launch this "jihad" of information-sharing. And I thank you, dear reader, for your "jihad" in taking the time to read it.

This book is intended for two types of readers: (A) Non-Muslims groping for answers to the troubling questions mentioned above; and (B) Muslims searching for reasons for the questionable behavior of some fellow Muslims. While attempting to satisfy the knowledge quest of such disparate groups within the same volume can be a dangerous exercise–with the danger of information overload for one group and inadequate information for the other–I hope the question-and-answer format employed will help keep alive the interest of both groups throughout the book. Please keep the following in mind as you read along:

(1) This book deals primarily with the Divine Message from God to the prophet Muhammad* (may peace be upon him), conveyed through the Qur'an, the Muslim holy book. I have used translations of the Qur'an by Abdullah Yusuf Ali (1989 edition) and Muhammad Asad (1980 edition). In the Qur'anic passages quoted, the materials appearing within parentheses represent the translators' effort to complete the meanings of these verses. My comments appear within brackets [ ].

(2) To show respect to God's prophets, Muslims add "peace be upon him" (shortened to "pbuh") whenever they mention a prophet's name. I am replacing "pbuh" by an asterisk (*), with the same reverence for all God's prophets resonating throughout the book.

(3) Other information source Muslims use, the *Hadeeth* (also spelled Hadith), are the <u>purported</u> actions and sayings of Muhammad*. While there are many beautiful Hadeeth which reinforce the Qur'an's message, others seem to run counter to the spirit of this Holy Book. How could these have crept into the sacred literature? Hadeeth are introduced in Chapter 1 and their relative strengths are discussed briefly in Chapter 3. Other terms related closely to Hadeeth are the *Sunnah* and *Shariah*. These are defined in the Glossary.

(4) When discussing Islam, people often compare the "ideals" of modern society with specific passages from the Qur'an or Hadeeth. For example, statements such as "Muslim men can have up to four wives and divorce them simply by saying 'I divorce you' three times," are not only subjects of non-Muslim criticism, but also are included in Western high-school and college textbooks without any discussion.

For objective analysis, such passages should be viewed in their socio-political context and also compared with corresponding passages in other sacred texts. I have attempted to do so by comparing these with relevant passages from the Hebrew Scriptures (<u>Tanakh</u>, Jewish Publication Society, 1985) and the Christian Bible (<u>The Holy Bible</u>, in King James Version, Dougan Publishers, Inc., 1985). Since passages similar to the Hebrew Scriptures quoted also are found in the Christian Old Testament, I am labeling these passages as Hebrew Scriptures/Old Testament. Corresponding passages from the Christian New Testament also are reproduced. To facilitate locating these and the Qur'anic passages quoted, I have indented them all. Additionally, to minimize the possibility of readers' taking the quoted Hebrew Scriptures/Old Testament and New Testament passages out of context, I have included brief explanatory notes by Rabbi Avi Magid of the Temple Emanu-El, Honolulu, and Regina Pfeiffer, Lecturer in Religious Studies and Assistant Director of the Master of Arts in Pastoral Leadership Program, Chaminade University of Honolulu. These appear immediately after the quoted passages. However, a few Biblical passages, added just before this manuscript went for printing and based on further study, unfortunately lack such explanatory notes.

(5) While background information on the Qur'an and Hadeeth is discussed in Chapters 2 and 3 respectively, readers are encouraged to read the useful commentaries by Gregg Kinkley and Regina Pfeiffer, included in the Foreword, on the Hebrew Scriptures/Old Testament and the New Testament passages included.

(6) Unlike passages from the above-mentioned Texts which I have quoted fully, I have often only summarized the main point(s) of each

Hadeeth quoted, with the Hadeeth compiler's name and Hadeeth number following immediately within parentheses.

(7) ☛ <u>Ijtihad</u>: Being troubled by the actions of some Muslims which I feel may run contrary to the spirit of Islam, I have, in many places, called for Ijtihad, or objective soul-searching by Muslims, to help us differentiate between behaviors that Islam preaches and the practices that some Muslims follow. In all such cases, a plea is made for us to "go back to the drawing board" and rethink these practices vis-a-vis the blueprint provided by God Almighty in the Qur'an. All such pleas for Ijtihad are identified with this pointer ☛. In some cases, I have also suggested Ijtihad by other groups (such as Jews, Christians, and Americans generally).

(8) Since this is by no means a definitive work but very much a work-in-progress, I would appreciate your comments to help improve the book's contents and effectiveness. Indeed, this writing is meant to stimulate the ongoing discussion on some generally ignored principles and teachings of Islam vis-a-vis the practices of some Muslims.

(9) My intent is not to hurt anyone's feelings but for all of us to move forward collectively as we grope for ways to turn around the foreboding of a *clash of civilizations* into a *congruence of civilizations.*

Please either write to me care of Moving Pen Publishers, Inc., P.O. Box 25155, Honolulu, HI 96825, USA, or visit our website <u>www.BeyondVeilAndHolyWar.com</u>.

May peace be upon you!

Saleem Ahmed, Ph.D.
Honolulu, Hawaii, USA
March 2002

ACKNOWLEDGMENTS

I wish to express my deep gratitude to many individuals whose feedback and support over the past eight years helped enrich significantly my thinking and writing. I should clarify that not all of my reviewers may have agreed with everything I've written; nor may I have accepted all their suggestions. Only I am responsible for the book's content. Although there are many overlaps, these individuals may be grouped into the following broad categories:

Individuals who provided substantive input and offered alternative viewpoints: Dr. Fida Muhammad Khan, Islamabad, who has also written a section of the book's Foreword; James E. Akins, former U.S. ambassador to Saudi Arabia, Washington, D.C.; Prof. Ayesha Jalal, History Department, Tufts University, Boston; Nizar Hasan, former President, Muslim Association of Hawaii; Atiqa Hachimi a sociolinguist from Morocco; Deborah Pope, Executive Director, Shangri-La, Honolulu; Asifur Rahman Tarique, a philosopher, poet, and writer, New Jersey; Dr. Everett Kelinjans, educator and former president, East-West Center, Honolulu; Prof. Wasim Siddiqui, retired professor and World Bank consultant; Mike Murphy, U.S. foreign service officer; Dr. Jerry Chang, President, HUG (Humanity United Globally), Honolulu; Linda A. Grzywacz, Development Manager, Honolulu Academy of Arts; Moana Tregaskis, writer and author of Hawaii; Ron Reddick, retired Peace Corps educator; Dr. Reynold Feldman of the international Subud movement; Air Vice Marshal (Rtd.) Nafees Najmi, Rawalpindi; Dr. Syeda Arfa Zehra, Lahore; Ruquia Jafri, educator, Dallas/Lahore, Shahla Zia, Esq., *Aurat* Foundation (NGO working for empowerment of women), Lahore; and Muzaffar A. Ghaffar, writer, Lahore. Also Saba Usman; Nuri Ronaghy; and Frank Gniffke, Esq., Honolulu; Michael Grainge, Georgia; and Shaukat Niazi, Islamabad, who also provided me several useful books to read.

Among my relatives I thank niece Sehba Shah and nephew Sayed Aule Saiyidain Shah, Lahore; nephew Qazi Ma'arijuddin, New York; and cousin Syed Musharaffuddin (deceased) who encouraged me to begin this writing project eight years ago.

In particular I thank my brother Akbar Ahmed and his children Saima and Hameed, Karachi; and my sister Dr. Firoza Ahmed and her late husband Air Marshal (Rtd.) A. Rashid Shaikh, Rawalpindi. Sadly, Rashid Shaikh, one of my strongest supporters, passed away as this manuscript was being finalized.

Individuals who helped improve my writing and highlighted passages that would be unclear to western readers: Barbara and Jack Oberholzer, Chuck Huxel, Rosamond and Jack Sullivan, Saltanat Siddiqui, Francis Rea-Welker, Dorothy Abreu, Marcia Dexter, and Julie Jow, all of Honolulu.

Individuals who have looked at the manuscript from a macro viewpoint in the light of contemporary developments and debate: Professor S. Cromwell Crawford, Chair, Department of Religion, University of Hawaii; and Professor Majid Tehranian, Director, Toda Institute for Global Peace and Policy Research, Honolulu/Tokyo and Professor, Department of Communication, University of Hawaii.

Individuals who over the past several years have encouraged me, often prodded me, to take the task to completion: Firdaus Akip, Singapore; Muqeem Khan, Sharjah; my brother-in-law Aslam Zafar, Rome; and Ather and Marivic Dar, Prof. D.P.S. Bhawuk, Dorothy Wheeler, and Lila Sahney, all of Honolulu.

Individuals who have critiqued the passages I have included from the Hebrew Scriptures/Old Testament and the New Testament: Rabbi Avi Magid of Temple Emanu-El, Honolulu; Gregg Kinkley, prayer leader and Ritual Committee chair for Congregation Sof Maarav, the Conservative Jewish synagogue in Hawaii; Pastor Sam Cox, United

Methodist Church, Kailua; and Regina Pfeiffer, Biblical Studies instructor, Chaminade University, Honolulu. Also I thank Gregg Kinkley and Regina Pfeiffer for writing the useful commentaries on their respective sacred texts, which have been included as part of the Foreword.

Individuals living in Hawaii who have helped me grasp the "core" of some religions discussed briefly in Chapter 4: <u>Baha'ism</u>: Florence Kelley; <u>Buddhism</u>: Rev. Thomas Okano, Director, Hawaii Institute of Buddhist Studies; Rev. Eshin Matsumoto; Rev. Kenjo Urakami; and Bishop Yubon Narashiba; <u>Daoism/Taoism</u>: Dr. Lily Chang, Daoist/Taoist Master; <u>Hinduism</u>: Inder and Terri Kapur; Dr. Raj Kumar; and Prof. Jagdish Sharma; <u>Jainism</u>: Harendra and Usha Panalal; and Usha Jain; <u>Sikhism</u>: Dr. and Mrs. Birendra Huja; and <u>Zoroastrianism</u>: Tehmasp, Katie, and Adil Kelawala and Dr. Meheroo Jussawala. For Confucianism and other religions, I have consulted various web pages.

Individuals who helped select the book's title: These include several of the above-mentioned people plus Joy and Mel Altman, Liz Bailey, Kuldip Bhogal, Al Bloom, Lib Clark, Arindam Chakrabarti, Bhagwan and Lavina Chatlani, Shashank Chitnis, Vincent Frederick, Nasir Gazdar, Carol Hanna, Janet Holman, Karuna Joshi-Peters, Elaina Malm, Vit Patel, Ijaz Rahman, Connie and Michael Riordan, the Rev. Renate Rose, Bithi and Jan Rumi; Arun & Meera Savara, Mohammed and Kohinoor Sayeed, Dipankar and Papia Sengupta, Sharad Shah, Miriam Sharma, Valerie and Bill Southwood, Connie and Nick Vikoulov, Joyce Vogler, and Indru & Gulab Watumull. These responses came from all over the world.

I specially thank my wife, Carol "Yasmin," who wore many hats, provided varied substantive and logistical assistance, put up with the mess in my room during all these years, and often played the devil's advocate; and my daughters Aisha and Seema and their respective husbands Dr. Dan Talley and Troy Hirsch, for being equally supportive and reviewing several drafts as the manuscript progressed through various stages over the past several years.

I acknowledge the love and understanding with which my parents, now deceased, raised me and the inquiring mind and respect for all religions they instilled in me. My elder sister, also deceased, Shirien Aslam Zafar, had a similar positive impact on me.

At the "institutional level," I thank the East-West Center, Honolulu, for its fellowship (1961-64), which not only helped me earn my Ph.D. degree but also broadened my perspective to appreciate other cultures and value systems. This opening of my mind forty years ago through the process of "mutual learning," is now being expanded further by the Open Table, an interfaith group which meets monthly in Honolulu.

Finally, I thank the Hawaii community for the warm aloha it extended to all Muslims and many non-Muslims who look like Muslims from Asia (such as Hindus and Sikhs) during the post-September 11th period, when stereotyping and hate-mongering unfortunately become commonplace in parts of the continental U.S. Without the peace of mind that comes from living in Hawaii, the completion of this manuscript probably would have been delayed indefinitely. Aloha!

Saleem Ahmed
Honolulu
March 2002

FOREWORD

1. A MUSLIM PERSPECTIVE

Islam is a religion of peace. In fact, the word "Islam" itself is derived from the Arabic root "SILM," which means peace. Moreover, the word used for the fundamental principles of Islam, generally known as the Articles of Faith, is IMAN, derived from the Arabic AMAN, which also means peace. Both words together suggest peace within and peace without. Thus a Muslim is called on both to be at peace within himself and to help create peace and harmony in the external world. The recent terrorist acts by individuals calling themselves Muslims, however, have given rise to many misunderstandings about the teachings of Islam. At the same time, the post-September-11th world has felt the need to know more about Islam. Indeed, since the airplane attacks, the Qu'ran itself has become something of a bestseller in the West. I am therefore pleased that Dr. Saleem Ahmed has written a book that should throw light on these topics and remove the misunderstandings that generally prevail in non-Muslim countries about Islam. One may not agree with all his views, but there is no doubt that he has provided an important service to those keen to learn more about Islam.

Having gone through an earlier version of this book, I am happy to find that Dr. Ahmed has incorporated some of my proposed changes even while sticking to his own point of view elsewhere. It is also encouraging to note that the present book contains many references to the Holy Qu'ran as well as such widely acclaimed source books of Ahadeeth as <u>Mua'ta Imam Malik</u>, <u>Sahih Bukhari</u>, <u>Sahih Muslim</u>, <u>Sunan Abu Daud</u>, <u>Sunan Al-Tirmidhi</u>, and <u>Fiqh-us-Sunnah</u>. No book on any religion will be universally accepted. Still, Dr. Saleem Ahmad deserves our thanks for his thorough scholarship.

In addition to Muslim sources, Dr. Ahmed makes generous use of quoted materials from the Hebrew Scriptures/Old Testament and the New Testament. This commendable feature shows his attempt to be unbiased and objective. Furthermore, a wide range of important subjects is covered, among them the Qur'an and Science; the Universality of God's Message; Jihad and Violence; the Status of Women; Marriage, Divorce and Inheritance; Adultery; Food, Drink, and Usuary; Slavery; Punishment for Crimes; Music, Dance, and Culture; and Reward and Punishment in the Hereafter. All this has been done in a question-and-answer format, which should make the information easily accessible to most readers.

Some of the views expressed by Dr. Ahmed will prove controversial among Muslims. An example is his ambivalence about the authority of Hadeeth, and his opinions on some other subjects may not be acceptable to everyone. But one must remember that every author has a distinctive social background, area of specialization, educational level, personal aptitude, and set of experiences, all of which will have a profound effect on the individual's thinking, understanding and formation of ideas. For a balanced outlook on any subject, one is well-advised not to be limited to a single viewpoint. In the case of Islam, moreover, it is very helpful if an individual has mastered the Arabic language in order to gain direct access to the original sources and not be compelled to rely on the available translations, which may limit the scope of one's understanding. The present work, in any case, is a sincere effort by Dr. Saleem Ahmed to present his opinions on some of the most important issues facing the Muslim world today. It is earnestly hoped that this book will provide guidance to all who are keen to benefit from Dr. Ahmed's enlightened and liberal views while gaining for themselves a greater understanding of Islam.

Dr. Fida Muhammad Khan
Visiting Professor of Islamic Law at various Pakistani Universities
Author, Mahfum al-Qur'an (The Meaning of Qur'an)
Islamabad, October 30, 2001

2. A JEWISH PERSPECTIVE

I can imagine no better time than now, nor a better messenger than my good friend Saleem Ahmed, to clarify and demystify the true purport of Islam and educate the non-Muslim world on its message as set forth in the Qur'an. Saleem's work is by its very terms as weighty an undertaking as it is important. Therefore none of us should feel ashamed or incapable from the outset of making an additional effort toward mutual understanding, which is clearly Saleem's goal. His intent–to bring people of all faiths closer together in peace through understanding–is totally consistent with the best of all three of the great monotheistic traditions: Judaism, Christianity and Islam. Rejoicing in our commonalities may well be the pre-requisite for future peaceful co-existence. One of those commonalities is that our shared traditions all ultimately rest on certain texts: the Jews have the Torah; the Christians the Gospels and the balance of the New Testament; and the Muslims the Qur'an. All faiths based on revealed texts over time interpret, re-interpret, amend, redact and indeed sometimes seem even to stray from their respective canons.

Traditions may differ on whether this sort of variance is healthy, natural, or perfidious, but no religion can truly represent that its texts have been followed to the letter and according to their surface meaning throughout all time. Thus it follows that no religion can be judged accurately simply by the tenor of its Urtext. To judge a text one must of course read and understand its purport; but I would assert that in our text-based creeds, simply reading the text is never enough–one must observe how the tradition in question has applied the text to actual situations and adapted those texts to inevitable change, whether through commentary, supplemental tradition, exegetical emendation or even straightforward amendment. A simple example from a more modern but equally text-based society should suffice. The United States of America prides itself on deriving its laws and principles from a single, unchanging document: the U.S. Constitution. The thoughtful textual researcher might easily conclude that, if we judge a people by its texts rather than its actions, racial bigotry is a principle of

American government since, in the Urtext of the Constitution, still encased in glass in the U.S. Archives building in Washington, DC., Article I. Section 2 restricts voting rights to "free persons" and sets the worth of non-free men and women at three-fifths of free individuals. Similarly, the exegete may be driven mad attempting to reconcile the 18th with the 21st amendments (Prohibition and its subsequent repeal), both codified within a text purporting to set forth only the broad and lasting principles of government.

The point I wish to make to the reader of this fine book is that all three Abrahamic faiths have gone beyond their sacred texts, even as they are still constantly informed and guided by them. Just as the parent remains in the heart and thoughts of the emancipated youth who was well and lovingly raised, so our texts and their memorized verses stick in our adult and emancipated consciences as we confront the ever-changing, novel phenomena of the moment, interpreting afresh as we all must how our textual guidance should be construed in this moment. Judaism, still well-described and defined by its sacred Torah, has also in a sense gone far beyond it—enough so that it would be unfair, or at the least misleading, to judge it totally on the basis of a few verses taken out of context and without the benefit of millennia of rabbinical gloss. Arguably, modern pharisaic Judaism is found as much in those glosses as in the unadorned and uninterpreted text. This is not "voodoo" ethics, but part of the road of learning and loving that the Holy One has set before us in His world of choice.

In sum, as Saleem exhorts us at the end of this work, let us not judge Islam by what some of its followers do but rather by what the Qur'an says. On the other hand, I would add, let us not judge Judaism by what the Torah seems to say in one or two verses quoted herein as the full reach of Jewish law encompassing the full range of human interaction. Jewish law was forced long ago to draw deeply from other wells, all as inspired as the original springs of Torah itself. With these thoughts in mind, the reader will be freed to consider both how praiseworthy the ethics of the Qur'an are, once read, and how difficult the task of applying word to deed is: a responsibility divinely conferred upon all our traditions, with our posterity's well-being held ever in the balance.

Salaam, shalom, and the healing wholeness of peace be with us all.

Gregg J. Kinkley
Prayer leader and Ritual Committee chair
Congregation Sof Maarav
The Conservative Jewish Synagogue
Honolulu, November 21, 2001

3. A CHRISTIAN PERSPECTIVE

If tolerance begins with understanding, understanding begins with dialogue. With the world today an increasingly global community, a paramount step to start the process toward tolerance is dialogue. We begin by learning about ourselves and others. In his text, Dr. Saleem Ahmed has initiated this process. He enters into a dialogue first within his Islamic community, then furthers the conversation with both the other Abrahamic traditions, Judaism and Christianity. He has selected to compare the rich scriptural foundations of the three traditions in significant areas of human life and in relationship to the one God that all three profess. Although each tradition has a particular understanding of that Being, all three share the concept that life is a gift from God, whether identified as Yahweh, the Trinity, or Allah.

The difficulty that arises is illustrated by the fact that while all three profess a single God and trace their roots to Abraham, they each have different languages and concepts to express their faith and relationship with God. Therefore, comparing the three traditions is a task as enormous as it is admirable. Through his scriptural comparisons, Dr. Ahmed strives to present a balanced representation of the three. In his preparation of this text, he has sought out passages from the Judaic and Christian Scriptures that respond to the questions he asks of the Qu'ran. First and foremost, though, Dr. Ahmed seeks the answers within his Islamic tradition before exploring how the other two view the same issues within their contexts. Although he quotes passages from the Bible that address the questions he raises, one caveat must be noted: all three traditions are conditioned by the specific time, place and people out of which they developed. Each must seek continually for the answers that renew and challenge, invite and inspire, seek and find peace for its adherents in the world of today.

Hebrew Scriptures/Old Testament, which began as an oral tradition, was not written or completed in much of its final form until after the Babylonian captivity, ca. 586 B.C.E. Some portions were written after this period. A later development in Judaism is in some ways similar to the Hadeeth. A commentary on the Scriptures emerges, what is known as the rabbinic teachings or oral teachings, compiled later into the Mishnah. These reflect on the meaning of specific passages of scripture. As an example, the Mishnah addresses the question of when it is acceptable to recite the evening prayers–at sunset, before dinner, after dinner, or before bed.

As I have said, Dr. Ahmed has taken on an enormous task, the success of which must be judged by you, the reader. Furthermore, is it possible for any of us to enter fully into a tradition that is not one's own? As a Christian, I realize that within my faith community there are many perspectives regarding several doctrinal issues that have led to disagreements and schisms within Christianity. As such, I believe there is no single answer to the questions posed by humanity. Instead, we are left with the necessity of asking the questions and the challenge–and beauty–of trying to answer them. Dr. Ahmed's book will help all of us–Jew, Christian, and Muslim alike–to find answers to many of life's most important questions.

Regina Rossi Pfeiffer, M.A.
Lecturer in Religious Studies and Assistant Director
Master of Arts in Pastoral Leadership Program
Chaminade University
Honolulu, January 15, 2002

CHAPTER I. SETTING THE STAGE
Muslim Beliefs, Information Sources, and Sects

I. MUSLIM BELIEFS

What does "Islam" mean? Who are "Muslims"?
Islam is the name of the religion. It means "submission to God" (*Allah* in Arabic). It provides followers with a "total way of life." Islamic worship encompasses certain beliefs together with righteous living. Followers of Islam are called "Muslims". While "Moslem" is an alternate spelling, perhaps "Muslim" is a more accurate transliteration.

What is the basic belief of Muslims?
Belief in God: Muslims believe in the One Almighty God. He is all-powerful, omnipresent, omniscient, and needs no rest. The entire universe may be considered to be but an atom for Him. He has neither ascendants nor descendants. We enjoy His presence everywhere. He is closer to us than our jugular vein. The Qur'an mentions 99 attributes of God, including mercy, kindness, and magnificence (Tirmidhi 2285; Appendix). He is the creator of life and death. He is supra-physical and formless. It would be erroneous to represent God in human form; we simply cannot comprehend Him. Perhaps we can feel Him by imagining that we are all surrounded by some "spiritual mist," which represents Him. This "mist" permeates through our bodies, similar to X-rays but with no harmful effect. Each molecule of Divine presence could be pictured as having "eyes" and "ears" together with an incredible "computer" to record all our actions.

We can picture our souls to be like iron filings which long to reattach themselves to that Great Magnet. Every time we do an evil deed, some "rust" forms on these filings; and every time we do a good deed, some rust is removed. When we die, the "net shine" left on our soul will determine whether we get attached to the Magnet.

God is not an arrogant and egocentric being who thrives on our worshiping Him. Rather, true worship comes from righteous actions. We are inspired to worship Him to help us get some of the rust removed from our souls. And, being omniscient, He knows whether our prayers, fasting, and pilgrimage are empty, hollow, selfish, and worthless rituals or righteous activities and true worship. God commands Muslims to have the following additional beliefs:

1. Belief in God's Angels: The Qur'an refers to them as "messengers with wings, two or three or four (pairs)," who carry back to God our souls when we die (Qur'an, chapter 35: verse 1). One angel each sits on either side of us (Qur'an 50:17) and records all our deeds (Qur'an 82:10-12). Angels execute what God commands them to do. Unlike humans, they apparently have no will power. The effect would be probably similar to what happens when we press command buttons, such as "cut" and "paste," on our computer keyboard: God says: "Do so-and-so," and the angels do it.

2. Belief in God's Prophets and His Books: The Qur'an informs us that God has sent prophets to all nations of the world (Qur'an 10:47; 16:36). And while 24 are named in the Qur'an, we are required to respect all–even those unnamed (see Chapter 4). According to Muslim tradition, God sent about 124,000 prophets the world over, from the beginning of human existence on this planet. God declares: "For each period is a Book revealed" (Qur'an13:38), with all Books carrying basically the same Message: "Serve God and shun evil" (Qur'an 16:36). The book revealed to Muhammad* is called the Qur'an, that revealed to Eesa* (Jesus*) is Injeel; to Dawood* (David*), Zabur; and to Moosa* (Moses*), Torah. In many cases, however, as the Qur'an states, God's message may have been probably misinterpreted by devout followers of these prophets.

Reinforcing the universality of God's message, the Qur'an also declares that Islam was actually founded by prophet Abraham* and completed under prophet Muhammad*. God describes Muhammad* as the "seal of the prophets" (Qur'an 33:40). Muslims interpret this to mean that he was the last prophet and that there will be no more prophets following him. This does not preclude the possibility of there being reformers in later times, who reinforce God's message and urge righteous living (Ali, 1989, page 1069, footnote No. 3731). This subject is also discussed in Chapter 4.

3. Belief in the Day of Judgment: God promises there will be a "Day of Judgment" (Qur'an 75:1-15), "when the sight is dazed, the moon is buried in darkness, and the sun and moon are joined together" (Qur'an 75:6-10). At that time we will all appear before Him, reassembled "in perfect order to the very tips of our fingers" (Qur'an 75:3-4) and will be answerable for all we did in this life. God will decide our reward or punishment based on the net of our good and bad deeds. No one else can intercede on our behalf.

The importance of these beliefs may be gauged from the fact that when people convert to Islam, they declare: "I believe in God, His angels, His prophets, His books, and the Day of Judgment."

The Qur'an also lays much emphasis on righteous actions. God asserts that worshiping Him is meaningless without righteous deeds such as honesty, discipline, hard work, tolerance, and modesty. He clarifies that He does not need our empty prayers and fasting. We will discuss the Muslim concept of good deeds in Chapter 5.

II. INFORMATION SOURCES USED BY MUSLIMS

From where do Muslims derive their guidance?
Muslims use two information sources:

1. The Qur'an: This is the compilation of God's message to prophet Muhammad*, revealed over a 23-year period. Muhammad* instructed his followers regarding the order in which the Qur'an was to be arranged and compiled in book form. The process of consolidation continued under the first two Caliphs (Muslim spiritual and temporal leaders– Khalifa in Arabic), Abu Bakar and Umar, and was completed

under the third, Uthman, about twelve to fourteen years after Muhammad* died. Based on God's assertion that the Qur'an is a "Tablet preserved" (Qur'an 85:21-22), Muslims believe this Book exists today in its original form–and that it will continue to remain as such in the future also. While interpretations may vary, the wording remains unchanged. Most of the time God refers to Himself in the Qur'an in the first person plural ("We", "Us", "Our"), although sometimes He also uses the first person singular ("I", "Me", "My").

2. Hadeeth: This is a collection of Muhammad's* purported sayings and actions, compiled some 250-300 years after he died–when he* was no longer available to confirm all that was being attributed to him. Technically, Hadeeth are a collection of the prophet's sayings; Sunnah are his purported actions; and Shariah is the codified version of Hadeeth and Sunnah. We will use Hadeeth to refer to all three. These run into several thousand and are discussed in Chapter 3.

Who wrote the Qur'an and when?
The Qur'an, Muslims believe, was revealed by the archangel Gabriel (Jib-ra-eel in Arabic) to Muhammad*, an "unlettered" Arab goatherd and caravan leader, from about 610 A.D., when Muhammad* was about 40 years old. Having many questions about spirituality and life, especially regarding the injustices of the rich and discriminatory treatment of women and slaves, Muhammad* apparently often went to a cave, called Hira, near his home town of Mecca, for meditation.

One day Gabriel suddenly appeared while Muhammad* was deep in meditation. Muhammad* was frightened and wanted to run away. But wherever he turned, Gabriel was there. Gabriel finally calmed Muhammad* and gave him the first revelation (Qur'an 96:1-5). After Gabriel left, the frightened and trembling Muhammad* hurried home and narrated the incident to his wife, Khadijah. He feared that perhaps he had gone insane. Khadijah assured him that he was still a sane person and became the first person to accept Islam as received by Muhammad*.

Gabriel returned many times, after long absences in earlier years but more frequently in subsequent years, to reveal other Qur'anic verses. It took 23 years for the entire Qur'an to be revealed. Muhammad's* followers would memorize the revealed verses and also write them down. Muhammad* modified his own actions to conform with the incoming revelations. For example, he changed the direction to face while praying from Jerusalem to Mecca on instruction from God (Qur'an 2:144), about 13 months after he* migrated from Mecca to Medina (Chapter 3).

Muhammad* started preaching the Message of One Supreme God who asked people to lead righteous lives and treat all humans, especially women and slaves, equally and with justice. The local pagan Arab chiefs started persecuting him as this preaching was against their beliefs and practices. However, Muhammad* continued to share the Message, in secret meetings during earlier years and in open meetings subsequently as he gained followers.

Why should I view the Qur'an as a message from God?
In addition to the substance of Muhammad's* message of belief in One God coupled with righteous living, the fact that this message, in beautiful, poetic, classic Arabic, could have come from the lips of an unlettered person is considered, in itself, a miracle by Muslims. However, for the modern analytical mind, probably the Qur'an's greatest miracle is the accuracy with which it revealed, more than 1,400 years ago, many natural phenomena which have only recently been "discovered" by science. These "predictions" are discussed in Chapter 2. Examples include creation of the universe from a single mass and its expansion (Qur'an 21:30), flotation of heavenly bodies in fixed orbits (Qur'an 21:33); aquatic beginning of life (Qur'an 24:45), and space flight (Qur'an 55:33). Following the Qur'anic assertion that some of its verses are to be taken literally and others allegorically (Qur'an 3:7), Muslims previously possibly assumed these revelations were to be taken allegorically. However, the scientific discoveries of only the past century have shown how accurate are these assertions made 1,400 years ago.

What is the importance of Hadeeth?
In the Qur'an, God has advised Muslims to seek clarification from Muhammad* on religious and temporal matters that may be unclear to them (Qur'an 4:59). Thus, people consulted the prophet often. After he died, people consulted his companions regarding what they remembered Muhammad's* response was on specific issues. After these companions also died, people consulted their descendants and so forth until about 250-300 years after the prophet's death, when his purported sayings and actions were compiled in book form.

Many Muslims consider Hadeeth to be as sacred as the Qur'an itself. After all, they contend, who would know how to interpret the Qur'an better than Muhammad*? Thus, some devout Muslims regard Hadeeth as a primary source of inspiration and information and unquestionably follow them in practically all aspects of life. However, some Hadeeth appear to me to not only conflict with other Hadeeth but, in some cases, even with the spirit of the Qur'anic message. Why? Their strengths and potential shortcomings are discussed in Chapter 3.

Who wrote these Hadeeth and when?
Most Hadeeth were compiled by devout Muslims from Central Asia about 250 to 300 years after Muhammad* died. Being concerned that the prophet's teachings might become distorted with time, they devoted many years and traveled widely seeking information on the prophet's actions from individuals whose ancestors had been companions of Muhammad*. The Hadeeth compiled by Al-Bukhari (died 256 A.H.), Muslim (d. 261 A.H.), At-Tirmidhi (d. 279 A.H.), and Abu Dawood (d. 275 A.H.) are the best known. The following three religious leaders, who lived even earlier, also compiled some Hadeeth; they also are respected as scholars of Fiqh or Islamic law: Imam Al-Shafie, Imam Malik, and Imam Ahmad ibn Hanbal. The compilations of An-Nassaie and Ibn Majah also occupy prominent positions. Of all these works, the compilation of Bukhari (known as Sahih Bukhari) is considered to be the most exhaustive Hadeeth collection (Alim, 1986). An even earlier writing on Muhammad's* life is the voluminous work of Ibn Ishaq (85-151 A.H.), Sirat Rasul Allah

(The Way of Allah's Apostle), which was edited by Ibn Hisham (d. 218 A.H.). I have consulted its English translation by Guillaume. Mahjul Balagha, a compilation of the Caliph Ali's letters and sermons, is an important information source for Shia Muslims.

III. SECTS AMONG MUSLIMS

How many sects are there among Muslims? How did they start?
The two main divisions are the Shias (or Shiites) and the Sunnis. The seed of discord was sown shortly after the prophet died. Since Muhammad* had not nominated a successor, a dispute arose regarding who should become the Khalifa (Caliph). Some favored Abu Bakar, Muhammad's* trusted companion and father-in-law; others favored Ali, the prophet's beloved cousin and son-in-law. Both had seen Islam grow through thick and thin, and both were very devout companions of the prophet. Following some sort of "election," Abu Bakar was chosen the Khalifa. Shias believe Ali should have been the first Caliph. Eventually, Ali also became Caliph, the fourth, after Abu Bakar, Umar, and Uthman, 20-25 years later. These four are called "pious caliphs". Except for Abu Bakar, the other three died of assassinations. With Ali's assassination in 661 C.E., the era of "pious caliphs" ended and that of Muslim dynasties started.

The division between Shias and Sunnis was sealed after Ali's son, Husain, was killed treacherously along with many companions at Karbala, Iraq, en route to Kufa (also in present-day Iraq), in 680 A.D. No Muslim condones what happened at Karbala. The difference is the importance attached to that event. Sunnis regard it as an unfortunate and tragic event; for Shias, it constitutes the basis for religious ritual. They mourn the tragedy and demonstrate their grief for 40-60 days every year. Sunnis consider such demonstrations against Qur'anic injunction, since the Book enjoins Muslims to be patient in suffering (e.g. Qur'an 2:153; 2:177). This difference of opinion also led to differences in the interpretation of the religion. For example, Sunnis consider Muhammad* and all subsequent community leaders to have been ordinary humans. Shias believe that Muhammad* and Imams (spiritual leaders) are "above" ordinary humans; they will follow their orders unhesitatingly. There also are many sub-sects among both Shias and Sunnis.

What does the Qur'an say about breaking into sects?

> Qur'an: (Do not be among) Those who split up their religion and become (mere) sects. . . . (Qur'an 30:32; also see 42:13-14; 43:64-65; 45:17; 45:28). [Many Qur'anic passages also narrate what happened to people who broke into sects (e.g. Qur'an 3:105; 19:37; and 45:28)].

> Hadeeth: Muhammad* apprehended and anticipated that his followers would also break into many sects (Tirmidhi 171).

I should clarify that some Muslim sects have produced wonderful, pious, progressive, and learned leaders. These sects are engaged in many proactive and progressive activities, especially in the rural areas of developing countries, for the betterment of society at large. They have established universities, hospitals, charitable institutions, and industries in many countries. Their leaders serve as wonderful role models. Because of the special relationship they enjoy with their followers, their role as positive change agents is highly significant. Their followers usually do not participate in violent activities.

Saleem, to which Muslim sect do you belong?
I do not belong to any sect. I seek guidance directly from the Qur'an plus those Hadeeth which complement the Qur'an. I am sorry for the injustices committed in the past in the name of religion. However, we cannot undo history. I want to move forward. Thus, rather than narrowing the definition of Islam through sects, I'd like to broaden it as that religion which epitomizes faith in a single God, respects equally all prophets of God, affirms the equality of all races, and requires the doing of righteous deeds.

CHAPTER 2. THE QUR'AN AND SCIENCE

Why should I believe the Qur'an is a divinely inspired book?
For the modern analytical mind, the "proof" that the Qur'an is a
Divine document must be derived inferentially from science. Thus let
us compare scientific views on the following 15 subjects with what the
Qur'an said 1,400 years ago. This chapter was inspired by Bucaille
(1976). Another good book on the subject is by Mahmood (1991).

I. CREATION OF THE UNIVERSE

1. Creation of the universe and its expansion
Scientific view: Up to the early 1930s it was believed, even by Albert
Einstein, that the universe was "static and stable." Then, in 1932,
Edwin Hubble discovered that all galaxies were "receding" from a
central point. The only way they could appear to do so, surmised
Hubble, would be if the universe were expanding like a balloon. If this
is indeed true, from what point did the expansion start? Scientists
could only conclude that the entire universe must have all been joined
together in a single mass at one point and then split apart, eons ago,
with such great force that this expansion is still continuing.

> Qur'an: The heavens and the earth were joined
> together before God split them apart (Qur'an 21:30).
> With power and skill We constructed the firmament.
> Verily it is We who are steadily expanding it (Qur'an
> 51:47). [Note: I am using Asad's translation for verse
> 51:47. Because there was no concept of an expanding
> universe when Abdullah Yusuf Ali was working on his
> translation of the Qur'an in the 1920s-early 30s, he
> translated this verse as "With power and skill did We
> construct the Firmament; for it is We who create the
> vastness of space."]

2. Contraction/destruction of the universe
Scientific view: The universe cannot expand indefinitely. Therefore, it will stop expanding at some point and then start contracting until it re-coalesces into a single mass.

> Qur'an: Humans ask: "When is the Day of Resurrection?" (It is) When the sight is dazed; the moon is buried in darkness; and the sun and moon are (again) joined together (Qur'an 75:6-9).

3. Re-creation of the universe
Scientific view: After the above-mentioned contraction and destruction, the universe may split again, to repeat another cycle of expansion and contraction. The current cycle may not be the first such cycle and probably won't be the last either.

> Qur'an: God begins the process of creation and repeats it (Qur'an 10:4).

4. Time it took to create the universe
Scientific view: Generally, the following six stages of creation are recognized: (1) Ionized Plasma; (2) Separation of Light and Matter; (3) Creation of primordial super galaxies; (4) Subdivision of the primordial super galaxies into galaxies and individual stars; (5) Creation of planets and moons; and (6) The present.

> Qur'an: We created the heavens and the earth and all between them in six ayam (Qur'an 50:38).
> [Note: Ayam (singular: yaum) means very long time periods. Just how long? Thousands of years long, as the following Qur'anic verses assert].
>
> The angels and the spirit ascend unto Him in a yaum, the measure whereof is (as) fifty thousand years (Qur'an 70:4). A day in the sight of your Lord is like a thousand years of your reckoning (Qur'an 22:47).

5. Motion of heavenly bodies

Scientific view: All heavenly bodies are "floating" in space in fixed orbits. Previously, it was believed, even by Einstein, that all heavenly bodies outside our solar system were static.

> Qur'an: All (celestial bodies) swim along, each in its rounded course. (Qur'an 21:33).

6. Space flight

Scientific view: The Wright Brothers flew 120 feet in 1903. Humans have now landed on the moon and may well be on their way to explore other planets, stars, and galaxies.

> Qur'an: O you assembly of jinns and men! Pass, if you can pass, beyond the zones of the heavens and the earth! But you will not be able to pass without authority (from God) (Qur'an 55:33).

> [Who are "jinns?" We don't know. God describes them as beings made "from fire free of smoke" (Qur'an 55:15). They are co-inhabitants of this universe with us.]

II. EVOLUTION OF THE EARTH

7. Stages in the Earth's evolution

Scientific view: After the cooling down of the initial molten mass (during the first two "days" of creation), the earth's evolution is divided into the following four geological stages: Archeozoic or Proterozoic, Paleozoic, Mesozoic, and Cenozoic Eras. Currently, we are in the Quarternary Period of the Cenozic Era.

> Qur'an: We created the earth in two days . . . and measured therein all things to give them nourishment in due proportions in four days (Qur'an 41:9-10)

8. Shape of the earth

Scientific view: We now know the earth is round. Even up to Christopher Columbus' time in the 15th Century, however, it was generally believed in the west that the earth was flat and that people could fall off the edge. By contrast, there is no concept in the Qur'an of the "four corners of the world," from where people could fall off.

> Qur'an: Travel throughout the earth and see how God did originate creation (for example: Qur'an 29:20). [The implication here is that there is no "edge" from which we may "fall off" the earth.]

9. Geological processes: Erosion of mountains

Scientific knowledge: It has only been within the last two centuries that geologists have concluded that mountains once stood in many places which have now been reduced to plains (referred to as "peneplains"). In the past, such a notion would have been ridiculed.

> Qur'an: They ask you concerning mountains. Say: "My Lord will uproot them and scatter them as dust. He will leave them as plains, smooth and level." (Qur'an 20:105-106).

10. Separation of sweet and salty waters

Scientific view: We generally believe that all ocean water is saline. However, it has been recently discovered that not only are there lenses of sweet water underlying islands such as the Hawaiian chain, but that such lenses may extend for several miles into the ocean. These lenses would be similar to the ocean current known as the Gulf Stream which carries warm ocean water from the Caribbean to England.

> Qur'an: It is He who has let free the two bodies of flowing water; one palpable and sweet, and the other salty and bitter; and He has made a barrier between them, a partition that is forbidden to be passed (Qur'an 25:53).

III. EVOLUTION OF LIFE

11. Aquatic beginning
Scientific view: It was only 150 years ago when Darwin proposed his theory of the evolution of species and also theorized that life evolved out of water.

> Qur'an: God has created every animal from water (Qur'an 24.45); It is He Who has created humans from water (Qur'an 25:54).

12. Male and female genders in all living matter
Scientific view: We have known all along that animals have been created in pairs, but now we also know that plants have male and female counterparts.

> Qur'an: Glory to God Who created in pairs all things that the earth produces, as well as their own (human) kind, and (other) things of which they have no knowledge (Qur'an 36:36).

13. Fertilization and embryonic development
Scientific view: The process of embryonic development has only been understood recently, through the help of modern techniques.

> Qur'an: We did create man from a quintessence; then we placed him as (a drop of) sperm in a place of rest firmly fixed; then We made the sperm into a clot of congealed blood; then of that clot We made a (foetus) lump; then We made out of that lump bones and clothed the bones with flesh; then We developed out of it another creature (Qur'an 23:12-14). I have fashioned him (in due proportions) and breathed into him My Spirit (Qur'an 15:29).

14. Sleep and death
Scientific view: Science does not yet have a clear understanding of sleep and death.

> Qur'an: It is God Who takes the soul at death. Those that die not, (He takes the soul temporarily) during their sleep. [But] Those on whom He has passed the decree of death, He keeps back (the soul from returning to life). The rest He sends (back to their bodies) for a term appointed (Qur'an 39:42).

15. Reincarnation
Scientific view: Science has not yet been able to provide us with any clue as to what happens after we die.

> Qur'an: We have decreed death to be your common lot, and We are not to be frustrated from changing your forms and creating you (again) in (forms) that you know not (Qur'an 56:60-61).

[Does this suggest reincarnation?]

☛ Ijtihad: How could an "unlettered" goatherd have arrived at all these scientifically credible conclusions? Only by divine inspiration is the answer given by devout Muslims.

Thus, Muslims believe that the Qur'an is indeed God's book. It could not have been written by Muhammad* or any other human. The Book merely records what was revealed to Muhammad* by Divine inspiration. And it has remained unchanged over the past 14 centuries.

IV. CREATION OF THE UNIVERSE IN OTHER BOOKS

Isn't the creation of the universe also covered in the Bible?
Yes it is. The following sequence in the process of creation is described:

Hebrew Scriptures/Old Testament: Day 1. In the beginning, God created the heaven and earth. The earth was without form and void; there was darkness; and Spirit of God moved upon the face of water. Then God created light and separated day and night. [The sequencing of other "milestones" in the creation process may be summarized as follows: Day 2: Heaven; Day 3: Earth and seas, vegetation; Day 4: Sun, moon, stars; Day 5: Birds, marine life; Day 6: Land animals, humans; Day 7: God rests] (Genesis 1.1-2.3).

Regina Pfeiffer's note: Translation from Hebrew to English varies in different English versions. The various translations for "heavens," for instance, include "skies" and "dome," but the main point is the separation of the waters above and the waters below. It corresponds to the fifth day and creation of birds and fish.

Undoubtedly the Author of the original message here must be the same as the Author of the message in the Qur'an. We don't know which Biblical prophet(s) received this message of creation. However, since the sequencing of "days" in the above-mentioned creation process is not scientifically accurate (for example, the earth being created before the sun), can we assume that changes may have occurred in the original message, possibly through misinterpretation by devout followers? Another example: if the sun was created on Day 4, how were the earlier three days measured (that is, without the sun being present)? Also, the definition of a "day" probably should not be taken literally, but, as the Qur'an declares, as a long time period.

What about other religions? For example, do not Hindus claim that their holy books also talk about creation in a scientifically accurate way?
I find that perfectly understandable. As discussed in Chapter 4, God informs us that He sent prophets to all nations of the world (Qur'an

10:47). All prophets carried the same message: Believe in One God and lead a righteous life (Qur'an 16:36). Since the process of creation of the universe did not change between books, all books of God would have discussed the same process, although the depth of explanation could have varied, depending upon the comprehension level of the people being addressed. I find this a most refreshing affirmation of God's declaration in the Qur'an that He sent prophets to all nations of the world. The universality of God's message is discussed in Chapter 4.

What about Hadeeth? Do they also discuss the creation of our earth? Yes. There are several Hadeeth on this subject. While many are vague, the following is noteworthy:

> Hadeeth: Muhammad* said: God created clay on Saturday, mountains on Sunday, trees on Monday, things entailing labor on Tuesday, and light on Wednesday. He caused animals to spread on Thursday and created Adam on Friday (Muslim 6707).

☛ Ijtihad: Would it be too far-fetched to "translate" Muhammad's* explanation into the following stages of the earth's evolution?

(1) "Clay on Saturday" would represent the initial breaking down of the earth's surface into rocks and their subsequent degradation into soil. This would correspond to the very long Archeozoic /Proterozoic geologic Era (from about 4.6 billion years to about 590 million years ago). This Era was devoid of life.

(2) "Mountains on Sunday" would represent the major tectonic activities that took place the world over and giving rise to our initial mountain chains during the Paleozoic Era, especially during the Cambrian through Devonian Periods. This lasted from about 590 million years ago to about 360 million years ago. This period had primary, simple life forms.

(3) "Trees on Monday" would correspond to the later part of the Paleozoic Era, especially the Carboniferous to Permian Periods of very large trees, from which most of our coal deposits are derived. This would have been from about 360 million years ago to about 200 million years ago, with primitive aquatic and other evolving life forms.

(4) "Things entailing labor [pains] on Tuesday" would probably represent the evolution of reptiles and mammals, during the Mesozoic Era (encompassing the Triassic, Jurassic, and Cretaceous Periods) and the early part of the Cenozoic Era (Paleocene through Pliocene epochs). This extended from about 200 million years ago to about two million years ago. The later part of this "day" was marked by much volcanic activity the world over during the Pleistocene Epoch of the Cenozoic Era, blanketing our planet's atmosphere with thick layers of dust for thousands of years, thereby preventing sunlight from reaching the earth's surface. The resulting lack of sunlight, widespread land subsidence and advancing seas, culminating in an Ice Age, would have caused most of the life forms to become extinct.

(5) "Light on Wednesday" would then correspond to the settling of the dust, re-emergence of sunlight on the earth's surface, retreating of polar ice caps, and evolution of most of the current life forms during the post-Pleistocene Period of the Cenozoic Era, from around two to one million years ago.

(6) "Animals spreading out on Thursday" would correspond to the early to mid Holocene Epoch of the Cenozoic Era, from about one million to 0.1 million years ago. During this time the earth was populated by all its varied animal and plant life forms that we find currently.

(7) Finally, "Creation of Adam" on Friday would represent the most recent phenomenon, taking place during the last 100,000 years or so and concluding with the evolution of humans during the late (ongoing) Holocene Epoch of the Quarternay Period of the current Cenozoic Era.

Is the creation of life also discussed in Hadeeth?
Yes. Many Hadeeth deal with the creation of life, but often in general terms. However, the following Hadeeth are noteworthy:

> Hadeeth: The prophet said: . . .The reproductive matter of a man is white and that of a woman is yellow. When the male's substance prevails, it is a male child that is created. And when the substance of the female prevails, a female child is formed (Muslim 614).

> Hadeeth: Muhammad* said: Everyone's creation starts with the collection of material for his body within the first forty days in the mother's womb. Then he becomes a clot of thick blood for a similar period (40 days) and a piece of flesh for a similar period. Then an angel is sent to him . . . and the soul is breathed into him (Bukhari 9.546).

☛ Ijtihad: Since the angel breathes God's Spirit into the embryo after 80 to 120 days, can abortion legitimately take place earlier, that is, during the time when the fetus is just a "lump of flesh," apparently without life? This possibility is supported by the tradition that Muslim funeral prayers are offered for a miscarried foetus if it is four months or older–and not if it is younger (Fiqh-us-Sunnah 4.46b). With our most sophisticated instruments, fetal heartbeat can be heard around the 18th week, sometimes as early as the 16th week.

☛ Ijtihad: How could Muhammad* have dreamed up this seemingly impossible dream related to the evolution of our planet? How could he* have known about the interaction between male and female chromosomes in fetal development and the time periods involved? Could all these have been possible without Divine inspiration?

CHAPTER 3. HADEETH:
Strengths and Shortcomings

As we learned in Chapter 1, since God advises Muslims to seek clarification from Muhammad* on all matters that may be unclear to them (Qur'an 4:59), many Muslims consider Hadeeth–the prophet's purported sayings and actions–to be as sacred as the Qur'an itself. Many regard Hadeeth as a primary information source and follow them unquestionably in practically all aspects of life. Muhammad* was so much respected and loved by his followers that they wanted to copy his way of life in every respect, even to the extent of knowing which leg to put forward first when leaving the mosque, in how many sips to drink water, etc.

What's wrong with that?
The potential problem was expressed by Muhammad* himself. He advised his followers to follow his actions and sayings only when these conformed with the Qur'an (Muslim 5830). He wanted to ensure that his followers did not mix up what he did as a human being with the Divine Message. Here is an example of an apparently incorrect advice he gave to some of his followers–and later acknowledged:

> Hadeeth: Once Muhammad* advised some fruit growers to change the way they grafted trees. They followed his advice, but their yield dropped significantly. On learning this, Muhammad* admitted: "You have better knowledge (of a technical skill) in the affairs of the world" (Muslim 5832).

It was thoughtful of Muhammad to have clarified this. So where's the problem?
Unfortunately there are instances where some Hadeeth not only conflict with other Hadeeth, but also with the spirit of the Qur'an.

Why should this have happened?
I believe the problem may have been caused by the procedure adopted in collecting Hadeeth.

What procedure was adopted?
As discussed in Chapter 1, Hadeeth compilers took great pains to ensure the testimonies they collected were genuine. They interviewed only individuals whose ascendants were known to have been honest and knowledgeable about the prophet's sayings and actions. This led to the establishment of the science of Hadeeth, which is a unique branch of Islamic study, esteemed by scholars internationally. Each Hadeeth consists of two parts: the *matan* (text, or substance) and the *isnad* (chain of reporters). Ideally, to be acceptable by our compilers, each Hadeeth had to meet the following five criteria (Azami, 1978):

1. Continuity in the chain of transmitters.
2. Integrity of the transmitters.
3. Soundness of memory of the transmitters.
4. Conformity of the Hadeeth with other Hadeeth on the same topic.
5. Absence of "defect" in the chain of transmission and/or in the text.

Do you see any problem here?
Yes. It seems our Hadeeth compilers gave more importance to the line of transmission (*isnad*) than to the substance (*matan*) of any account. In other words, we find here an over-emphasis on <u>process</u> at the expense of <u>substance</u>. Thus, for example, the compilers accepted the Hadeeth that the prophet ordered adulterers to be stoned to death, disregarding the fact that the Qur'an does not prescribe death for adultery. It prescribes 100 stripes and permits adulterers to marry others "similarly guilty" after receiving this punishment (Qur'an 24:2-3). This obviously means that the guilty must survive the punishment –which will hardly be possible if they are stoned to death. And while our Hadeeth compilers assert that stoning is meant for married individuals, the Qur'an does not differentiate between illegal sex committed by single and married individuals.

What, in your view, are the strengths of Hadeeth?
Hadeeth serve an invaluable function of describing methodology to be followed at important religious events such as birth, marriage, and death; prayers, fasting, and pilgrimage. Hadeeth are indispensable for this purpose as these rituals are not described in the Qur'an.

And what might be some shortcoming in some Hadeeth?
The following appear to me to be some possible shortcomings with which we are confronted. These are not listed in any order of priority.

Shortcoming No. 1: Possible memory lapse. Some companions of the prophet, who may have been in their teens and 20s when Muhammad* died, may have lived for 50+ years after his death. Could they have suffered memory lapses? Let us remember there were only a few literate people in the world 1,400 years ago. Consider the following:

> Hadeeth: One of the prophet's companions, when asked to narrate some incident [apparently several years after the prophet had died], responded: "I have grown old; I have almost reached the end of my life span and have forgotten many things in connection with the prophet. So, accept whatever I narrate to you, and those which I do not narrate, do not compel me to narrate" (Muslim 5920).

> Hadeeth: Umar Ibn Hasin, another companion of the prophet, who was conscious of the treacherousness of memory, said that, while he could relate the prophet's actions for a long time, he does not do so because he was afraid of "hallucinating." He explained that someone else (whom he does not name) has recounted events which are different from what he himself recalls (Mernissi, 1991, page 79).

Shortcoming No. 2: Possible innovations: Could some companions of the prophet or their descendants have tried to gain personally by making changes in Hadeeth–even "inventing" new ones–to please rulers or cause harm to others, especially women? Ishaq (d. 151 A.H.), who is considered to be the earliest writer on the prophet's life and whose work survives today, introduces us, on page xv of his book, to Shurahbil bin Sa'd, a companion of the prophet, who, "in his old age . . . would blackmail his visitors: if they did not give him anything, he would say their fathers were not present at (the Battle of Badar)." Indeed, apprehending the possibility of innovations in his Sunnah, Muhammad* had already declared:

> Hadeeth: Whoever revives a Sunnah which dies after I will be rewarded in the Hereafter; and whoever introduces some evil innovation, which was not approved by God or His messenger, will be punished (Tirmidhi 168).

Fatima Mernissi (1991, page 49) cites the following Hadeeth as another example of possible innovation:

> Hadeeth: When the Persian king Kisra died, the prophet inquired "Who has replaced him?" The answer was: "His daughter." The prophet then reportedly observed: "Those who entrust their affairs to a woman will never know prosperity" (Bukhari 5.709, 9.219).

Mernissi explains that the originator of this Hadeeth was Abu Bakra (not Abu Bakar, the first Caliph). She explains that Abu Bakra narrated this Hadeeth to Caliph Ali, about 25 years after the prophet had died, and after Ali's victory over the army headed by Aisha (one of Muhammad's* widows), in what later came to be known as the "Battle of Camels." That battle was fought because Aisha was disappointed that Ali was not prosecuting the people considered responsible for the murder of the third Caliph, Uthman. Mernissi wonders whether Abu Bakra was trying to win Ali's favor by rationalizing, 25 years later, why Ali should be the leader of Muslims and not Aisha. [Incidentally, this Hadeeth highlights that, during the early period of Muslim history, women could rise to high positions, including being the commander-in-chief of the army]. Mernissi also wonders (page 61 of her book) why was this Hadeeth even included in Bukhari's compilation? After all, Abu Bakra had been flogged earlier by the second Caliph, Omar, for falsely accusing a woman of having an illicit sexual relationship–and was, therefore, no longer qualified to provide testimony. The Qur'an declares:

> Qur'an: Those who launch a charge against chaste women and do not produce four witnesses (to support their allegations), flog them with eighty stripes and reject their evidence ever after (Qur'an 24:4).

Far from degrading women, the Qur'an not only emphasizes the equality and reciprocity in male-female relationships (see Chapter 7), but it also reminds us of the prosperous and magnificent kingdom of Queen Saba (apparently the Biblical Queen of Sheba), and describes her conversion to Islam under prophet Solomon (Qur'an 27:22-44).

Mernissi also introduces us to another companion of the prophet, Abu Hurayra, who perhaps recounted the largest number of Hadeeth (about 5,300)–and all based on his two years' association with the prophet. In contrast, the number of Hadeeth recounted by some other individuals, having much longer periods of association with the prophet (18+ years), is as follows: Abu Bakar (later, the first Caliph): 142; Umar (the second Caliph), 537; Ali (the fourth Caliph), 536; and Aisha (Muhammad's wife) 2,210 (http://www.submission.org). Also, many Hadeeth narrated by Abu Hurayra were not witnessed by anyone else. This in itself becomes a very contentious issue as the usual rule adopted by our Hadeeth compilers in most other cases was to accept Hadeeth only when there were two or more independent witnesses. (See Azami's rule No. 4, quoted on page 46).

Mernissi raises many questions about Abu Hurayra's integrity and points out that Aisha, the prophet's widow, often disputed his Hadeeth. Aisha once said, "Abu Hurayra, you relate Hadeeth that you never heard." Abu Hurayra responded, "All I did was collect Hadeeth while you were too busy with kohl (eye makeup) and your mirror" (Mernissi, page 72). On another occasion, some people heard Abu Hurayra report:

> Hadeeth: Muhammad* declared: "He whom the dawn finds sullied [by the sex act] may not fast." These people then asked the prophet's widows (Aisha and Umm Salama) for verification. The latter responded: "The prophet used to spend the night sullied without making the ritual of purification and in the morning fasted." When these people subsequently confronted Abu Hurayra, he confessed that he had not heard this directly from the prophet but from someone else (Mernissi page 73; also narrated in Muwatta 18.11, with summaries in Muwatta 18.10 and 18.12).

Mernissi reports another incident of misogyny–also reported by Abu Harayra–as follows:

> Hadeeth: Muhammad* stated: "Three things bring bad luck: house, woman, and horse." When Aisha heard, she clarified as follows: "Abu Hurayra came to our house when the prophet was in the middle of a sentence. He only heard the end of it. What the prophet said was: 'May God refute the Jews. They say three things bring bad luck: house, woman, and horse'" (Mernissi pp 75-76). Similar cases of misogyny are found in Bukhari 7.30 and 3.826, and clarified by Aisha in Bukhari 1.486, 1.490, 1.493

Shortcoming No. 3: Communication distortion: We all are aware of how communication might get distorted when a message is transmitted from one person to a second to a third and so on. Imagine the extent of communication distortion that might take place when a message is transmitted by people spread across eight to ten generations, and over a period of about 250 years. True, we are talking here about the deeds of an extraordinary person, but the communicators of this message, companions of the prophet and their descendants, were ordinary people, like us. Even Matthew, Mark, Luke, John, and other writers of the New Testament recalled different events of Jesus Christ's* life, and that was not long after Jesus*' short physical life. Differences and contradictions are also found in the Hebrew Scriptures/Old Testament. For example, while the Ten Commandments declare: "Thou shalt not kill" (Exodus 20:3-17), it also directs the Hebrews to: "slay the Amalekites . . . both men and women, infant and suckling . . ." (1 Samuel: 15:3). (Chapter 6).

True, we have examples of some oral traditions, such as the Hawaiian tradition, which were passed across several hundred years, unchanged. However, these were recorded in chants and songs. That did not happen with Hadeeth, although it did happen with the Qur'an. Since the Qur'an is often recited in beautiful musical style, literacy is not required for it to be passed on across generations. But Hadeeth were not similarly transmitted. And, as we saw earlier, literacy was not very high 1,400 years ago.

Shortcoming No. 4: No knowledge of when an event occurred: Since many Hadeeth are undated, we do not know when various incidents described therein took place. Let us remember that Islam was not static during the 23 years of Muhammad's* prophethood: it changed with each revelation. For example, he* changed the direction to face while praying from "the heaven" [which most commentators believe means Jerusalem] to Mecca on receiving Divine guidance (Qur'an 2:144), about 13 months after he migrated from Mecca to Medina (Abu Dawood 507). Although Muhammad* was a very honest and spiritual person, probably he had no prior knowledge of what was going to be revealed to him. The Qur'an reminds us:

> Muhammad is no more than a messenger (Qur'an 3:144).

The prophet also admitted his dependence for guidance on the revelations he received:

> Hadeeth: "Someone asked me about such and such things about which I had no knowledge until God gave it to me" (Muslim 614).

> Hadeeth: "I intended to prohibit cohabitation with a suckling woman until I considered that the Romans and the Persians do it without any injury being caused to their children thereby" (Muslim 3391).

While Muhammad* would change his actions to conform to incoming revelations, this would, unfortunately, not get reflected in any earlier Hadeeth on the subject–although subsequent Hadeeth would carry the new incident. The problem would be similar to aliens visiting Earth in the 1960s and reporting back that Americans practiced racial discrimination and South Africans practiced apartheid. Other aliens, from the same planet, visiting us 40 years later would report the opposite. If both reports were undated, readers would not know which one to believe. Similarly, when an obese person loses 100 pounds weight, his snapshot taken earlier would still show him at his previous weight. Consider the following "mixed signals" due to different time periods being involved. These pertain to temporary marriage (mut'a):

> Hadeeth: (a) Muhammad* declared, "If a man and a woman agree (to enter into temporary marriage), their marriage should last for (at least) three nights. And if they would like to continue (their marriage), they can do so; and if they want to separate, they can do so" (Bukhari 7.52; also Bukhari 6.139 7.13a, and 7.51).

> (b) However, Ali (later, the fourth Caliph), clarified: "God's Apostle forbade mut'a on the day of the battle of Khaibar (628 A.D.), and he also forbade the eating

of donkeys' meat." (Bukhari 9.91, 5.527, 7.50, 7.432;
Abu Dawood 2068).

Which Hadeeth do we follow? Fortunately, since the second Hadeeth
carries a date, we can conclude that mut'a was permissible until the
Battle of Khaibar, or for about 18 years after Muhammad* started
receiving revelations. However, since the Qur'an only forbids eating
pork, the second Hadeeth probably predates the Qur'anic verses
dealing with dietary restrictions (for example, Qur'an 2:172-73). The
complexity of this and several other issues may be gleaned from the
fact that mut'a is still practiced among some Shias in Iran and
elsewhere (Ruquia Jafri, personal communication). (See also Chapter
8). Thus, primary reliance upon Hadeeth may result in conflicting
viewpoints.

Fortunately, in some Hadeeth Muhammad* provides an explanation
for why he is rescinding his previous advice:

> Hadeeth: Some person went to Muhammad* and said,
> "We have a food shortage. I have nothing to feed my
> family except some donkeys. But you have forbidden
> us to eat donkeys' meat." Muhammad* responded:
> "Feed your family donkey's meat. I forbade this earlier
> because these animals feed on the filth of the town"
> (Abu Dawood 3800).

As touched upon in Chapter 1, a more serious matter is penalty for
adultery involving married people. While this penalty is generally
believed to be stoning the guilty to death (*rajam*), the Qur'an
prescribes 100 stripes to both parties and stipulates that they should,
thereafter, be allowed to marry only others who are "similarly guilty"
(Qur'an 24:2-3). Isn't it possible, therefore, that Muhammad* initially
followed the Jewish tradition of stoning adulterers but changed his
position after he received guidance that the punishment was to be 100
stripes? (See Chapter 9). After all, God declares:

Qur'an: If any do fail to judge by (the light of) what
God has revealed, they are (no better than) those who
rebel (Qur'an 5: 47).

Shortcoming No. 5: No knowledge of an event's context: According
to some Hadeeth, adulterers were to be stoned to death; but,
according to another, however, they were to be first whipped 100
times and then stoned to death. And in still another case, Muhammad*
reportedly wished that an adulterer, who had escaped but was caught
and killed, could have been permitted to escape (see Chapter 9). Do
these reflect differences in the context (in addition to differences in
the time periods involved)? But since many Hadeeth do not describe
the context of events, which do we follow?

Shortcoming No. 6: Editorial judgment of the Hadeeth compilers:
During the 20-plus years of his research, Bukhari reportedly collected
more than 300,000 accounts. But his compilation contains only about
7,500 Hadeeth, or 2.5% of his collection. Also, since many Hadeeth
are repeated under different headings, it appears that Bukhari lists only
about 2,230 separate incidents, or less than 1% of his original
collection. What happened to the remaining 297,000 Hadeeth?
Bukhari explains that he excluded many because he questioned the
authenticity and integrity of some narrators and/or their ascendants.
But since Bukhari interviewed only those people whom he had already
"screened" and found to be honest, isn't it possible that he excluded
some Hadeeth because he could not believe that the prophet could
have done such-and-such thing or made so-and-so statement? What
was excluded? We will never know.

Shortcoming 7: Incomplete coverage of the prophet's life: How much
of the prophet's life is recorded in Hadeeth? If we assume that it took
the prophet approximately one hour on average to complete each
reported action or saying (the range being from a few minutes to
several days), the 2,230 incidents reported by Bukhari would have
required 2,230 hours, or less than 200 days (assuming a day to have
12 hours of "wake time"). Muhammad's* prophethood lasted 23

years, or approximately 8,400 days. Thus, he had a total of approximately 101,000 hours of "wake time" available. The above-mentioned 2,230 hours of "accounted wake time" would have taken less than 3% of Muhammad's* total available wake time. Even if we add the Hadeeth compilations of all compilers, these will probably account for less than five to 10% of the prophet's time. What did the prophet do in the remaining time? Could some of this have been represented by the reports that Hadeeth compilers excluded?

Shortcoming No. 8: Considering Muhammad's* actions and sayings as sacrosanct: Muhammad* often emphasized to his followers not to take as sacrosanct all that he did and said in his capacity as a human being. Consider the following Hadeeth:

> Hadeeth: Some people were quarreling at the door of Muhammad's* dwelling [apparently after he had given a verdict]. He came out and said: "I am only a human being. Opponents come to me (to settle their problems). Maybe some of you can present your case more eloquently than others, and I may consider him true and give a verdict in his favor. So, if I give the right of a Muslim to another by mistake, then it is really a portion of (Hell) Fire [for the one who wrongly accepts it]" (Bukhari 3.638).

> Hadeeth: And, as we saw earlier, Muhammad* admitted to some fruit growers that they had "better knowledge (of a technical skill) in the affairs of the world" (Muslim 5832)

What in your view is the position of Hadeeth vis-a-vis the Qur'an? While the Qur'an was revealed to Muhammad* through Divine inspiration, written during his life, and confirmed by him, Hadeeth are human compilations of Muhammad's* reported sayings and actions, compiled some eight to ten generations after he* had died and was no longer available to confirm them. Thus all kinds of inaccuracies, accidental or intentional, could have occurred. It is unfortunate that, while Hadeeth compilers apparently laid much emphasis on the chain of transmitters, little or no attention seems to have been given to the substance of transmission, that is, to assess the extent to which any purported Hadeeth conformed to any Qur'anic injunction on the subject. No wonder Muhammad* emphasized the following:

> Hadeeth: A person is not to be obeyed when it involves disobedience to the Creator (Tirmidhi 3696).

☞ Ijtihad: Wouldn't "disobedience" occur when someone does something contrary to the Qur'an–such as killing someone for adultery when the Qur'an prescribes 100 lashes and permits the guilty to marry other similarly guilty thereafter (covered in Chapter 9)?

Have such serious shortcomings in Hadeeth been discussed earlier? Yes. Possible innovations in Hadeeth were recognized even shortly after the prophet's death. In the Introduction to Ibn Ishaq's book (pp. xiv-xlvii) we are provided with a flavor of the "human-ness" of Hadeeth transmitters; of their biases as they filtered information to favor one line of thinking over another. Mernissi's accounts (1991), discussed on previous pages, provide us with further disquieting information on the character of some important Hadeeth transmitters.

Discussing the opposing contentions of those who want to preserve Hadeeth at all costs and those who want to reject them, Fazlur Rahman (1966, page 67) states: "The disentanglement of the historical prophetic elements is perhaps incapable of complete achievement for want of early sources. But a candid and responsible investigation into the development of the Hadeeth by the Muslims themselves is a desideratum of the first order. Whatever can be achieved will be a sheer gain, for it will reveal the intimate connection between the community and the prophet on the one hand, and between the doctrinal and the practical evolution of the community and the growth of the Hadeeth on the other. It will illuminate the relationship between these three and will clear the way for proper future development."

What should Muslims do in matters where Hadeeth reports seem to contradict the Qur'an?
I believe Muslims should follow those Hadeeth which complement or clarify some Qur'anic injunction. Those who seem to run counter to the spirit of the Qur'an are perhaps best ignored. As we saw earlier, fearing that enemies of Islam might introduce questionable practices as "authentic" Hadeeth, the prophet had advised:

> Hadeeth: Whoever revives a Sunnah which dies after I will be rewarded in the Hereafter; and whoever introduces some evil innovation which was not approved by God or His messenger, will be punished (Tirmidhi 168).

And what should Muslims do in matters not covered by the Qur'an or Hadeeth?
They should do Ijtihad (soul-searching). Consider the following conversation between Muhammad* and Muadh ibn Jabal, who was being sent to Yemen as ambassador and teacher of Islam:

> Hadeeth: The king of Yemen requested the prophet to send some scholars to teach Islam. The prophet commissioned a group of competent missionaries and made Muadh ibn Jabal their leader. The prophet asked Muadh: "According to what will you judge?" "According to the Book of God," replied Muadh. "And if you find nothing therein?" "According to the Sunnah of the prophet of God." "And if you find nothing therein?" "Then I will exert myself (exercise Ijtihad) to form my own judgment." Muhammad* was pleased. . . . The prophet personally bade farewell to this mission of guidance and light, and walked for some distance alongside Muadh as he rode out of the city. Finally, he said, "O Muadh, perhaps you will not meet me again after this year. Perhaps when you return you will see only my mosque and my grave."

Muadh wept. Those with him also wept. A feeling of
sadness and desolation overtook him as he parted from
his beloved prophet. The prophet's premonition was
correct. The eyes of Muadh never beheld the prophet
after that moment. The prophet died before Muadh
returned from Yemen. There is no doubt that Muadh
wept when he returned to Medina and found there was
no longer the blessed company of the prophet.
(Biography of Muadh ibn Jabal, in Alim, 1986).

Doesn't this touching account also capture Muhammad's* "human
side"–a side we do not usually see from many Hadeeth?

Can you cite some other Hadeeth you feel may be incorrect?
Yes. Consider the following:

Hadeeth: Some people of the tribes of 'Ukl and 'Uraina
came to the prophet and embraced Islam. Since they
found Medina's climate unsuitable and fell ill, the
prophet suggested they stay with the prophet's camel
herder and drink camels' milk and urine (as medicine).
Later, they killed the prophet's camel herder, reverted
to heathenism, and drove away with the camels. After
they were caught, on the prophet's order, their eyes
were branded with pieces of iron, their hands and legs
were cut off, and they were left in the desert till they
died (Bukhari 1.234, 5.505, 7.623, 8.794, 8.796,
8.797, and 9.37).

Two serious problems arise: (1) Drinking camels' urine. Nowhere in
the Qur'an is there even a hint of using animal urine for any
purpose–let alone for drinking. This would violate the Islamic concept
of purity. [Note: Some devout Muslims suggest that, since camels'
urine contains uric acid, it might have had a beneficial effect on some
ailments at that time. While this response may be true, it highlights
that these Muslims are willing to go out of the confines of the Hadeeth

to seek a valid explanation. I wholeheartedly support this strategy but suggest that we adopt a similar strategy–of Ijtihad–with other questionable Hadeeth as well. Incidentally, doesn't human urine also contain uric acid?] (2) The cruel nature of the punishment. Muhammad* was known as a kind and compassionate person. Thus, could he have really inflicted such cruel punishment on anyone, even if the criminals had perpetrated a similar torture on the camel herder they killed (we don't even know whether they did that)? While the Qur'an permits "eye for an eye, and a tooth for a tooth" in retaliatory punishment, it adds that "it is better to forgive" (Qur'an 2:178; 5:45; 42:40). Moreover, Muhammad's* life is full of forgiveness, not vengeance. Thus, can this Hadeeth be accurate?

Thus, is it important to know whether purported acts of Muslims are based on the Qur'an or on questionable Hadeeth?
Yes indeed. This will help clarify many troubling questions that non-Muslims have about Islam. For example, acts of terrorism and sexism, the practice of head-to-foot veiling of women, and the cancerous Shia-Sunni infighting, are not based on the Qur'an (see subsequent Chapters). However, we should also remember that there are many Hadeeth which are foundational in the exposition of the Qur'an.

Are there any Hadeeth that you follow?
There are many. For example:

> Hadeeth: Muhammad* advised: Avoid inflicting the prescribed penalty on Muslims as much as you can, and if there is any way out, let a man go. For it is better for a leader to make a mistake in forgiving than to make a mistake in punishing (Tirmidhi 3570).

Isn't this beautiful? Unfortunately, some Muslim religious leaders try to show how "religious and pious" they are by becoming increasingly more intolerant, rigid, authoritarian, and myopic. They seem to believe it is better to make the mistake of inflicting the most serious punishment possible than finding a way to forgive the person. While such narrow-minded and intolerant people are found among followers of other religions as well, that should hardly be a consolation and excuse for our own questionable actions.

How might devout Muslims who model their lives on Hadeeth respond to your serious questioning about their validity?
Let me emphasize that I am neither inventing any new Hadeeth nor rejecting all existing ones. There are many beautiful Hadeeth, many quoted in this and subsequent chapters, that I follow wholeheartedly. However, others possibly need much soul-searching. Even here, my intention is not to hurt anyone's feelings but to help initiate Ijtihad.

To those devout Muslim men who believe that all Hadeeth represent the prophet's* actions to clarify Qur'anic verses–and must therefore be followed unquestioningly–let me ask: Is your first wife older than you (Khadija was about 20 years older than the prophet*)? And is only one of your other wives previously unmarried (as was Aisha in the prophet's case), with others being divorcees or widows (as were all other wives of the prophet*)? And since the prophet* reportedly had 13 wives, why don't you? Why stop at four? (See Chapter 8 on rules governing marriage, divorce, circumcision, and inheritance). And to those devout Muslim men and women who similarly believe that all Hadeeth must be taken as accurate and followed to the letter, I ask: Do you drink camels' urine for any ailment (as was reportedly suggested by the prophet*, per Bukhari 1.234, 5.505, 7.623, 8.794, 8.795, 8.796, 8.797, and 9.37) (see pages 58-59)?

Let me conclude this chapter by suggesting that the first allegiance of Muslims should be to the Qur'an. The Hadeeth are a wonderful repository of guidance for Muslims– if they are used responsibly and sensibly–keeping in mind possible shortcomings.

☞ Ijtihad: How shall we deal with those Hadeeth which seem to conflict with other Hadeeth–and possibly also with the spirit of the Qur'an?

CHAPTER 4. UNIVERSALITY OF GOD'S MESSAGE

I. THE NAMED PROPHETS

Isn't Islam highly intolerant of other religions?
No. Some Muslims might be, but Islam is not. Islam is a very tolerant, universal, and broad-minded religion. It asserts that God sent prophets to all nations of the world–all of whom are to be respected equally:

> Qur'an: To every people was sent a messenger (10:47; 16:36); God sent messengers among all people with the command: "Serve God and shun evil" (16:36); To those who believe in God and His messengers and make no distinction between any of the messengers, God will soon give their reward (4:152; 2:285); and Nothing is said to you (O Muhammad) that was not said to the messengers before you (41:43).

The Qur'an reinforces this concept by declaring unequivocally that God's reward is for all believers, regardless of their religion:

> Qur'an: Those who believe (in the Qur'an), and those who follow the Jewish (scriptures), and the Christians, and the Sabians–any who believe in God and the Last Day and work righteousness – shall have their reward (Qur'an 2:62) [See Glossary for Sabians].

How does this Islamic concept compare with what the Hebrew Scriptures/Old Testament and New Testament say on the subject?
Unlike the above-mentioned Qur'anic concept, the only way to reach God, according to the Hebrew Scriptures/Old Testament and the New Testament is through their respective belief systems:

Hebrew Scriptures/Old Testament: When the Lord
your God shall deliver them [seven nations mentioned]
to you, you will smite them and utterly destroy them.
You will make no covenant with them nor show them
any mercy. . . . For you are a holy people. . . .You will
be blessed above all other people. . . . (Deuteronomy
7:1-26). And the Lord has avowed this day. . . to
make you high above all nations which He has made.
. . (Deuteronomy 27:17-19).

(Rabbi Magid's note: The Hebrew Scriptures was
written for Jews and concerning how Jews are to
worship. Its negative attitude toward other gods has to
do with idolatry alone. It says nothing about
Christianity and Islam. True, post-Biblical tradition has
a great deal to say, but that requires much discussion.)

(Regina Pfeiffer's note: One of the key difficulties
about the concept of religious tolerance and how the
Hebrew Scriptures/Old Testament look upon other
religious traditions is that these scriptures were written
during a period of time in which monotheism was in an
early, developing stage among the Near East
traditions. Texts from the ancient Near East,
predominantly polytheistic, present a portrait of gods
that differ from the later Hebrew writings. The threat
perceived by the inspired writers is that often the
people of their time would abandon the one God. To
prevent that, the natural reaction is to assert the
correctness of the Judaic tradition, that God has
chosen the people to bring the message of one God
and right living in response to that one God.)

New Testament: I am not sent but to the lost sheep of
the House of Israel (Matthew 16:24). He that believes
in him [Jesus] is not condemned; but he that believes
not in him is condemned already because he has not

believed in the name of the only begotten Son of God (John 3:18).

(Regina Pfeiffer's note: The Christian Scriptures are grappling with a question of what our relationship with God is in and through Jesus, how do we understand ourselves as a community of God in relationship with Judaism in particular and with other religious traditions such as Roman and Greek in general.)

Then, does the Qur'an recognize Jesus and Moses as prophets?
Yes. The Qur'an describes Jesus* as the "Spirit of God" because God breathed His Spirit into Mary for his birth (Qur'an 21:91); and Moses*, as the one to whom God spoke directly (Qur'an 19:51-53).

Who else are named in the Qur'an as God's prophets?

> Qur'an: God did, afore time, send messengers before you (O Muhammad). Of them, there were some whose story God has related to you, and some whose story God has not related to you (Qur'an 40:78).

While God sent prophets to all nations, only the following 24 are named in the Qur'an, 20 of whom are also mentioned in the Bible:

Biblical name	Qur'anic name	Biblical name	Qur'anic name
Adam	Aadam	Aaron	Haroon
Noah	Nuh	Elias	Ilyas
Abraham	Ibrahim	Elisha	Al-Yasa
Enoch	Idrees	Lot	Loot
Ishmael	Ismail	___	Hud
Isaac	Ishaq	___	Shuaib
Jacob	Yaqoob	___	Salih
David	Dawood	Ezekiel	Dhul-Kifl
Solomon	Sulaiman	Zechariah	Zakariyah
Job	Ayoob	John	Yahya
Joseph	Yusuf	Jesus	Eesa
Moses	Moosa	___	Muhammad

Then in which ways does Islam differ from Judaism and Christianity?
There are many similarities based on all three being monotheistic
religions. So, at the risk of appearing to oversimplify the Message, I
would summarize the main differences as follows:

Differences between Hebrew Scriptures/Old Testament and Qur'an
> a) Tribal God versus universal God: In the Hebrew
> Scriptures/ Old Testament, Yahweh is projected as the
> God of the Hebrews only; in the Qur'an, God is
> projected as the God of all humanity, with ranking
> among humans in His eyes being only through our
> respective degrees of righteousness (Qur'an 49:13).
> (Rabbi Magid's note: In the Jewish tradition, Yahweh
> seems to go back and forth between a particularly
> Jewish and a more universal focus).
>
> b) Chosen people versus equality of people: In the
> Hebrew Scriptures/Old Testament, the Hebrews are
> projected as the "Chosen People" of Yahweh, to
> whom Yahweh promised a homeland. In the Qur'an,
> all humans are projected as being equal, with no
> special privilege or land assigned to any group because
> of ethnicity, class, or any other characteristic. The
> Qur'an asserts that all humans have the same
> opportunity to attain paradise: "The most honored of
> you in the sight of God is (the person who is) the most
> righteous" (Qur'an 49:13).
> (Rabbi Magid's note: In the Jewish tradition, the
> "chosen-ness" in general had to do with responsibility,
> not privilege).
> (Regina Pfeiffer's note: While the people of Israel are
> "chosen people," they are also the "light to the
> nations" and have a specific responsibility to bring all
> people to the one God, Yahweh. So, while you have
> correctly asserted that in the Hebrew Scriptures/Old
> Testament, the people of Israel are chosen by God to

be in a special covenantal relationship, the writings also express that this relationship requires adherence to moral obligations and rules, such as care for the widow, orphan and stranger in one's midst).

c) Prophethood of Jesus*: Jews do not consider Jesus* to have been a prophet; the Qur'an, on the other hand, describes Jesus* as a prophet and the "Spirit of God."

Differences between the New Testament and Qur'an
(a) Son of God versus prophet: The New Testament looks upon Jesus* as the Son of God; the Qur'an looks upon him as a prophet, while recognizing his immaculate conception. The Qur'an asserts: "No son did God beget, nor is there any god along with Him" (Qur'an 23:91).
(Regina Pfeiffer's note: Jesus is also described as a prophet. For example, "The things that happened to Jesus the Nazarene, who was a prophet mighty in deed and word . . ." (Luke 24:19).

How do you explain Qur'anic passages which are anti-Jewish?
Two "types" of "anti-Jewish" passages exist: (1) "Philosophical": The "Children of Israel" are reminded by God of His favors and how they turned against Him (e.g., Qur'an 2:40-86). (2) "Operational": Relations of Muslims with Jews and Christians changed with time. Thus, God's advice to Muslims changed from a warning to not take them as friends (Qur'an 5:51), through improved relations with Christians–but still a warning to not trust Jews (because they reneged on their promise to help Muslims in a particularly important battle with the pagans, Qur'an 5:82)–to declaring both Jews and Christians to be "People of the Book" and encouraging Muslims not only to befriend them but also to intermarry with them and share food with them (Qur'an: 5.5). Chapter 6 discusses this more fully.

But doesn't Qur'an explicitly command Muslims to kill Jews?
No Qur'anic passage urges Muslims to kill anyone–Jews, Christians, hypocrites, or pagans. It permits taking up arms only in self-defense and to counter oppression. See Chapter 6.

II. THE UNNAMED PROPHETS

If God sent prophets the world over, why are others not named in the Qur'an?
It is believed traditionally that God sent about 124,000 prophets the world over (Fida Muhammad Khan, personal communication) and throughout human history. With such a large number, where should have been the cutoff point in naming them in the Qur'an? With the limited knowledge of world geography 1,400 years ago, it probably would have only confused people to learn of prophets in places they had not heard of. We can assume that God chose to narrate the stories of only those prophets with whose names the Arabs might have been perhaps already familiar through Judaism and Christianity. After all, Muhammed* was a descendant of Abraham*.

Who might be some unnamed prophets?
I include holy men and women of various religions who preached about One God and righteousness and who were bestowed with a Book by the Creator. While in some cases their books may have been misinterpreted and changed by devout followers, this should not belittle their prophetic offices. First, let us look at how some of these holy men described the Almighty and/or showed us the path to reach Him:

1.   This holy man preached three tenets–good words, good thoughts, and good deeds–as the pathway to reach the Almighty, whom he described as the Supreme Spiritual Light.

2.   This holy man listed right conduct, right knowledge, and right belief as the essentials needed for the perfection and purification of the soul and for reaching Him.

3.   This holy man described the Supreme Being as the one who appointed the emperor as the father of his people, to rule with piety and virtue and help alleviate human suffering.

4.   This holy man said: "There was something mysteriously formed, born before Heaven and Earth, quiet and still. Pure and Deep. It stands on its own and does not change. It can be regarded as the mother of Heaven and Earth. I do not know its name. I call it _____."

5.   This religion describes the Supreme Being as follows: "He has no set form, but can manifest Himself in any form. Though we describe His attributes, yet He has no set attributes, but can manifest Himself in any and all excellent attributes. . . . Being formless and without substance, He has always been and will always be. It is not a physical body that must be nourished; it is an eternal body whose substance is Wisdom. He has neither fear nor disease. He is eternally changeless. . . . His body fills every corner of the Universe; it reaches everywhere; it exists forever regardless of whether we believe in Him or doubt His existence."

6.   This religion describes the Supreme Being as follows: "He is the Omniscient Lord. He is not born; He does not die. Smaller than the smallest, greater than the greatest, He dwells within the hearts of all. Though seated, He travels far; though seated, He moves all things. Formless is He, though inhabiting form. In the midst of the fleeting, he abides forever. He is all-pervading and supreme."

☞ Ijtihad: Don't these descriptions of the Almighty appear to be similar to passages in the Qur'an describing God's various attributes (see Appendix)? Could these philosophers and sages conjure up the abstract concept of this Supreme Being without inspiration from that same Supreme Being? True, devout followers of these holy men may have misinterpreted the message in later years. But should that lessen the importance of the original message of these messengers?

Who are these holy men?

1.   Zoroaster* (founder of Zoroastrianism, c. 628-551 B.C.E., born in Persia). He described *Ahura Mazda*, the God of Good, who will eventually prevail. Zoroastrians pay homage to *Ahura Mazda* through fire, which represents to them the Supreme Spiritual Light. This, to me, reinforces the Qur'an's description of God as "light upon light" (or purified light) (Qur'an 24:35). The Zend-Avesta is the sacred scripture of the faith.

2.   Vardhamana Mahavira* (last reformer–*Tirthankar*–of Jainism, 599-527 B.C.E., born in India). He refers to the Supreme Being as *Jina*, and their sacred text is called Sutraji.

3.   Confucius* (Also known as Kong Zi*, founder of Confucianism, c. 551-479 B.C.E., born in China). Among his books were the Analects and The Great Learning.

4.   Lao Zi* (founder of Daoism/Taoism, 6th. Century B.C.E., born in China). He calls the Supreme Being as *Tao/Dao*." Lao Zi* is best known for the Tao Te Ching (Dao De Jing).

5.   Gautama Siddhartha* (the Buddha) (founder of Buddhism, c. 563-483 B.C.E., born in current-day Nepal). He expounded the Noble Eightfold Path needed to reach the ultimate state of peace: right views, right intentions, right speech, right action, right livelihood, right efforts, right mindfulness, and right concentration. The *Eternal Buddha's* description quoted above is from Bukkyo Dendo Kyokai, 1997, pp. 48-52. The Buddha's* chief text might be the Dharmapada, or Way of the Dharma. [Note: While I take the term "Enlightened Buddha" to refer to Gautama Sidharta*, I take "Eternal Buddha" to refer to God].

6.   The unnamed Hindu Rishi(s)* who described *Bramh*, as quoted above, around 1,500 B.C.E. (The Upanishads. Prabhavananda and Manchester, 1957, pg. 18). The same sage(s) also implored people to lead righteous lives characterized by duty and devotion.

Other inspired scriptures of Hindus include the <u>Bhagavad Gita,</u> <u>Ramayana</u>, and <u>Mahabharata</u>. [Note: *Bramma*, a deity, is not the same as *Brahm*, the Almighty].

But what about people who lived before these prophets were born? Are they all condemned because they did not worship the Almighty?

> Qur'an: For each period is a Book (revealed) (Qur'an 13:38). Mankind was [at one time] one single nation (Qur'an 2:213).

A just God would not punish "pagans" who worshiped other objects simply because no one had conveyed God's message to them. Thus, God reassures us that He sent prophets to all nations and throughout human history–starting from Adam*, at which time humanity was a single nation. Shouldn't we therefore also include among God's prophets unnamed sages of other peoples, such as Native Americans, African tribes, Australian aborigines, ancient Europeans, Pacific Islanders, et al., who may have similarly spoken of the One Supreme Being and enjoined people to lead righteous lives? In many cases, however, their followers may have forgotten the original message and started worshiping these sages and/or physical objects. Since the earliest prophets lived in pre-literate times, their "message" would have been disseminated through stories, chants and dances.

But in Buddhism, Confucianism, and Daoism, don't followers worship/invoke their respective founders?
None of these holy men asked their followers to worship them. However, the piety, compassion, and "spiritual enlightenment" they expounded have been so powerful that followers, out of reverence, seek their founder's blessings. Such tendencies appear to be common to many religions and belief systems. Even among Muslims there are some who deify Muhammad*; others deify other Muslim personages as well. For example, it is a common practice among some Muslims to visit the graves of Sufis and other holy men and invoke them. Isn't the fine line between reverence and deification being crossed here?

In the case of Buddhism, Confucianism, and Daoism, since the "Supreme Being" remains beyond comprehension (as He does also in Islam), the path to achieve salvation has been considered traditionally to be through seeking the founder's blessing. It is noteworthy that none of these religions describes their founder as God; in all, he is considered to be a master, teacher, or an enlightened one. Thus, wouldn't these founders be similar to the Islamic concept of Muhammad*, Jesus*, and Moses*?

And how do you reconcile polytheistic Hinduism with monotheism? Let us consider the following note by Inder Kapur explaining to us how Hinduism is monotheistic.

MONOTHEISM IN HINDUISM *(By Inder Kapur)*

Hinduism is the oldest and the most misunderstood religion. It pre-dates Judaism, Christianity, and Islam, not to mention Jainism, Buddhism, and Sikhism, which are all offshoots of Hinduism. Unlike other major religions of the world, Hinduism has no [known] founder like Moses, Jesus, Muhammad, or Buddha. The Hindus also do not base their faith on one single book like the Qur'an or the Bible.
A commonly misunderstood aspect of Hinduism is that it is a polytheistic religion–that Hindus believe in many deities, while Muslims and Christians, for example, believe only in one God. This is an oft-repeated charge against Hinduism. Nothing could be further from the truth, however.

If one looks even casually at the Vedas or the Upanishads, which constitute the most sacred texts of Hindus, it will become clear that Hindus believe in One reality as the underlying cause of all creation. All plurality is in the manifestation of that Reality. All divisions are on the surface. Deep down it is the same ocean–the ocean of consciousness.

Vedanta really means Bhedanta; the end of all Bhed, or division. "Ekam satyam Vipra Bahudha vadanti. Ekam satyam bahudha kalpayanti," says the Veda. There is only one reality, which the wise spell in many ways; one truth they contemplate in many ways. "The One that has become many" is the refrain one finds often in the <u>*Vedas*</u>.

According to Hindu understanding, the causal stuff of this universe– the raw material from which this universe is made–is consciousness. This creation is consciousness-based, "chetna janya." And this consciousness has taken a billion forms. It lies dormant in what we call inanimate matter like stones and hills. It is a bit more alive and awakened in trees and plants, and even more alive in the animal kingdom. It dwells in its purest form at the core of the human being as what the Upanishads call "Atman," soul or spirit, which constitutes the true nature of man. That "Atman," which is "anandi anant," (without beginning, without end, and eternal), is no different from "Parmatman," or God. In fact, the two are one and the same. That reality is what made the Vedic Rishis proclaim, "Tat-twam-asi," "Thou art that."

An interesting point to note here is that the "utpatti stahn" of the Universe–the point of origin–is both the "Chetna stahn" and "Anand stahn:" The source of the Universe is the same as consciousness and bliss. It has dual qualities. It is both the source of consciousness and the source of joy. That is why when we touch the source, we experience such indescribable joy, "Anand". God has been called "Sat-chit-anand" (eternity, consciousness, joy) in Hinduism. The God of Hinduism, however, is not a person. This "God" is the metaphysical essence of all reality. The difference is between a "divine person" and "divine reality." The Hindu God is not some kind of a creator who sat somewhere and one day created the Universe. The image is not of a potter making a pot or a painter creating a painting. It is more like a dancer, indistinguishable from the dance. If one separates the pot from the potter or the painting from the painter, the pot and the painting will still exist. But if you separate the Hindu God from its creation or if divinity goes out of creation, creation will cease to exist. The Hindu God as creator and its creation are not separate entities. Creation is God. "Isha-Vasya

Idam, yat kinch jagatyam jagat, " says <u>Isho-Upanishad</u>. This creation is permeated with divinity. There is no dance possible without the dancer and no dancer possible without the dance. Both are inseparable.

The Hindu God is neither compassionate nor loving in the sense that God in other monotheistic religions is. Such attributes could be assigned only to a person, even though a divine person. What Hinduism then says is that if there is love and compassion in life, it must have a source. That source is God. God is the source of everything. God is that source from which compassion and love flow.

God, according to Hinduism, is that power from which everything has emerged. The same power or source from which everything has emerged also sustains it, and eventually it will dissolve itself into the same source. And the process of emergence and submergence goes on endlessly: It is eternal, without beginning and end.

Hindus worship God in many ways, in all God's manifestations. The genius of Hinduism lies in its ability to dissolve and synthesize all surface plurality into one single unifying whole named Bramh–the source of everything. Hindus contemplate and worship Bramh in all its manifestations which by its very nature is diverse and plural. Besides, if the same Bramh or God is in everyone and everything, then hatred should not be possible. Who is one going to hate? The same divinity dwells in all creation. Thus, the idea of converting others to their own religion never occurred to Hindus. If God exists even in trees and stones and I worship them, how can I ever think of committing violence against those trees, let alone a fellow human being? This is what gave birth to the idea of non-violence, as enunciated by Jainism and Buddhism in the past and people like Mahatma Gandhi in modern times.

A question is sometimes asked that if Hinduism believes in one reality then what about all these innumerable gods and goddesses ? What about idol worship? There are many explanations for idol worship that do not conflict with the concept of One reality. First of all, the various gods and goddesses represent different aspects of divinity. Secondly, if God is in everything, then why not in a tree, in a river, or even in a stone. To a Hindu every part of creation is sacred, even a snake. So Ganga [Ganges], the river, becomes a goddess, tulsi, a plant, is a goddess. Besides, for the average person, it is easier to focus on an object than on an abstract concept. But a Hindu understands that ultimately all these various gods and goddesses merge into that one underlying reality called 'Bramh', which encompasses all. Divine in Hinduism is contemplated as the One in many and the many in One. Bramh in whom 'all find one nest'. 'He is the One, the One alone, In him all Deities become One'. Says the well known Vedic scholar, A.C. Bose, "in form the Deities are many, but in spirit they are One." "Vedic henotheism (a term coined by the well known German scholar, Max Mueller, to describe Vedic concept of God) is an expression of this spiritual approach".

Note: Inder Kapur is a journalist, writer, and poet from India. He currently lives in Honolulu, Hawaii, and writes on such diverse subjects as politics, social issues, and spirituality.

☛ Ijtihad: Doesn't Inder Kapur's view of monotheism in Hinduism get reinforced by the following Qur'anic verse?

> Qur'an: To every people have we appointed rites and ceremonies which they must follow. Let them not then dispute with you on the matter. But invite (them) to your Lord, for you are on the Right Way (22:67).

Let us compare how Hindus and Muslims pray:

The Hindu practice: Depending upon the blessing needed, Hindus pray to a specific deity. For example, for increased wealth and/or children, they pray to the goddess Lakshmi; for health, to the god Subramaniam; for knowledge, to the goddess Saraswati; and for good luck and protection while traveling, to the god Ganesh.

The Muslim practice: For receiving similar blessings, Muslims turn to a specific attribute of God (from among His 99 attributes. see Appendix). Thus, when they want wealth, many Muslims recite "Ya Razzaq" (the Provider) hundreds of times; for health, it is "Ya Salaam" (Source of Peace); for protection against calamities, it is "Ya Hafiz" (the Preserver); and for children, it is "Ya Khaliq" (the Creator), "Ya Bari" (the Evolver), and/or "Ya Musawwir" (the Fashioner).

While praying, Muslims try to focus on "nothingness" and Hindus, on images. Since focusing on "nothingness" is difficult, some Muslims focus on the image on their prayer mat, usually that of the Ka'bah, or the word "Allah" (God) written in Arabic calligraphy. Even then, the mind may wander. To avoid such loss of concentration, devout Hindus, centuries earlier, gave each attribute of the same God a specific physical form to help remain focused while praying. Thus, as Inder Kapur explains, when they pray, Hindus are not praying to that particular "piece of clay" but to the attribute of God it represents. And isn't it noteworthy that even these creative Hindus could not create an image suitable to describe the Supreme Deity, *Bramh*, with all His attributes? [Note: *Brahm*, the Supreme Creator, is different from *Bramma*, a deity].

☛ Ijtihad: Don't Muslims pray around the Ka'bah and kiss the Black Stone embedded in it–and refer to these rites as remembrance of God and not idol worship (Chapter 5)? So, if a Hindu prays in front of an image and calls it remembrance of God, who are Muslims to say it is not so?

☛ Ijithad: Just as humans evolved unique languages over centuries, they also evolved unique ways of remembering the Almighty–molded to a large extent by their respective socio-physical surroundings. For example, ancient people living in volcanic areas saw Him in fire; and seafaring people saw Him in the sea and the wind. Shouldn't Muslims marvel at these ancient sages who introduced specific attributes of God to their respective communities? Shouldn't Muslims see the same God everywhere? Shouldn't Muslims see here an affirmation of the Qur'anic assertion that He sent prophets to all nations of the world?

III. RELIGIOUS INTOLERANCE

Aren't Muslims highly intolerant of other religions?
Some zealous Muslims are, but Islam is not. As we saw earlier, Islam recognizes the prophets of many religions. Unfortunately, we find intolerant people among followers of all religions.

Then what makes Muslims so narrow-minded that if a Muslim converts to any other religion, he or she faces death?
Such actions are <u>not</u> based on the Qur'an. As we saw earlier, the Book declares unequivocally the freedom of religious choices that all of us have. "Let there be no compulsion in religion" (Qur'an 2:256). The Qur'an does not even hint that apostates are to be harmed in any way:

> Qur'an: Those who turn back as apostates after guidance was clearly shown to them, have been instigated by the evil one and buoyed up with false hopes (Qur'an 47:25).
> [But there is no Qur'anic passage suggesting any punishment to apostates].

Why are Christian missionaries prohibited from engaging in proselytizing activities in some Muslim countries?
Such prohibition, I feel, is an insult to the Qur'anic assertion "Let there is no compulsion in religion" (Qur'an 2:256). It also reflects an unnecessary sense of insecurity about their religion among these Muslims. By encouraging people to travel around the world and understand what happened to people who did not follow God's Message (Qur'an 12.109), God wants people to follow His Message only after careful investigation.

☛Ijtihad Since Muslims can preach Islam freely in non-Muslim countries, shouldn't non-Muslims have reciprocal rights in Muslim countries? How else can Muslims claim that their path is the "best" unless people can objectively discuss the question "compared to what?"

What about the destruction of the Buddha* statues in Afghanistan?
This destruction by the Taliban in Afghanistan in March 2001 cannot be condoned. The Taliban justified their action by explaining they merely followed the prophet's example who destroyed the idols found inside the Ka'bah (Bukhari 2.671, 5.584). But those idols were "illegal occupants" in that House, built by Abraham* and Ishmael* for the Worship of One God. Those idols had been placed there later by the descendants of Abraham* after they reverted to heathenism. In contrast, the Buddha's* statues had been carved out of sheer rock, in wilderness, out of devotion, sincerity, and love for the Buddha*; they were not "illegal occupants" in any house. Not only did the Taliban action show a complete lack of respect for other people's beliefs, it also destroyed irreplaceable cultural artifacts.

The destructions of Buddha* statues in Afghanistan by extremist Muslims and the destruction of a Muslim mosque in India by extremist Hindus are unfortunate examples of religious intolerance by zealots. Messages of such intolerance and hate are <u>not</u> found in either religion.

IV. RECENT RELIGIOUS REFORMERS

How do you look upon recent religious leaders and reformers such as Guru Nanak, Baha'ullah, and Mirza Ghulam Ahmad?

<u>Guru Nanak</u> (1469-1538, born in India) preached monotheism and exhorted his followers to lead righteous lives. His movement was a response to the then prevailing Muslim and Hindu practices such as intolerance and caste division. The political powers at that time considered his reformist ideas a political threat and started persecuting his followers. Sikhism was declared a separate religion approximately 60 years after Nanak's passing away. <u>Guru Granth Sahib</u>, the Sikh holy book, describes God as follows: "There is only one God. He is the Creator, Sustainer and Destroyer" (Guru Nanak, Var Majh). "The Formless Supreme Being abides in the Realm of Eternity. Over His creation, He casts His glance of grace. In that Realm are contained all the continents and the universes, exceeding in number all count. Of creation,

worlds upon worlds abide therein; All obedient to His will; He watches over them in bliss, and has each constantly in mind" (Guru Nanak, Japji). "He neither has father, nor mother, nor sons nor brothers" (Guru Nanak, Maru).

☞ Ijtihad: Aren't these passages similar to the Qur'an's description of God? Shouldn't Muslims, therefore, look upon Guru Nanak as a Sufi, a Master, who reaffirmed God's message–at a time when Muslims apparently had stopped following His message?

Baha'ullah: (1817-1892, born in Iran) preached about the unity of God, the universality of His message, religious tolerance, and righteousness. He declared himself to be the "new messenger" predicted by the Bab (see below). However, since the Qur'an describes Muhammad* as the "Seal of the prophets"(Qur'an 33:40), it is unthinkable that any other person, especially a Muslim, should claim himself to be a prophet. Thus religious leaders considered his preaching blasphemous and exiled him. The Baha'i faith was thus born. Prior to this, the same religious leaders had executed Mirza Ali Muhammad (1819-1850) (known as The Bab), who proclaimed that he was the "gateway" to the "Hidden Imam," a new messenger of God who was to come (which Baha'ullah subsequently claimed to be).

The movement that Mirza Ghulam Ahmad (1835-1908, born in Qadian, India) started, followers claim, is an embodiment of the benevolent message of Islam: peace, universal brotherhood, and submission to the Will of God in its pristine purity. The movement encourages interfaith dialogue and tries to correct misunderstandings about Islam. It advocates love and understanding among followers of different faiths. Many Muslims also consider Ahmad's claim of being the Divine Messiah blasphemous. Although there now are two sub-sects, with one of them denying that Mirza Ghulam Ahmad made any claim of prophethood, the sect has been excommunicated in some Muslims countries. Followers are called Ahmadiya or Qadiani.

☛ Ijtihad: God describes Muhammad* as the "Seal of the Prophets" (Qur'an 33:40). Thus, if someone else claims to be a prophet, shouldn't I let that be settled between that person and God? Shouldn't I learn from the good things he or she may say about morality and righteousness, and ignore things that I may disagree with? Shouldn't I follow the Qur'anic advice: "To you, your way, and to me, mine" (Qur'an 109:6)?

V. SUMMING UP

On the whole, how does Islam look upon other religions?
The Qur'an celebrates religious pluralism. The Book reminds us that the name of God is commemorated in many houses of worship:

> Qur'an: If God had not checked one set of people by means of another, [then] monasteries, churches, synagogues, and mosques, in which the name of God is commemorated in abundant measure, would have been pulled down (i.e., destroyed) (Qur'an 22:40).

Nowhere in the Qur'an does God describe Himself as "God of the Muslims"; it is always "God of all Creation" (Qur'an 1:2); He is "the God" of all humanity. He makes no distinction among humans on the basis of ethnicity, geography, social status, gender, or language. All humans have equal opportunity to reach Him directly, without any intercessor. The Qur'an declares unequivocally:

> Qur'an: The most honored of you in the sight of God is
> he who is the most righteous (Qur'an 49.13).

This is exactly the opposite of the impression of Islam in the West. What should Muslims do?

> Qur'an: Invite (all) to the Way of your Lord with wisdom
> and beautiful preaching; and discuss with them in ways
> that are best and most gracious (Qur'an 16:125).

CHAPTER 5. DUTIES OF MUSLIMS

What duties are Muslims required to fulfill?
They are to fulfill their duties to God, fellow humans, and self.

I. DUTIES TO GOD

In Chapter 1, we were introduced to the Muslim Article of Faith: Belief in God, His angels, His prophets, His revealed books, and the Day of Judgment. God has endowed humans with the intellectual capacity to understand, the soul and conscience to be good and righteous, and feelings to be kind and humane. And while He does not need anything from us in return, He asks us to know and love Him and to show our gratitude to Him by fulfilling our duties to others and self.

II. DUTIES TO FELLOW HUMANS

What is the relationship between duties to God and to fellow humans?
Islam describes fulfilling duties to others as worship and emphasizes that the only way to reach God is through righteousness, asserting further that empty rituals of worship are meaningless gestures.

> Qur'an: The most honored of you in the sight of God is (he who is) the most righteous (Qur'an 49:13).

How do you define "righteousness"?

> Qur'an: It is not righteousness that you turn your faces toward East or West; but it is righteousness to believe in God, the Last Day, the Angels, the Book, and the Messengers; to spend of your substance out of love for Him for your kin, for orphans, for the needy, for the wayfarer, for those who ask, and for the ransom of

slaves; to be steadfast in prayer; to practice regular charity; to fulfil the contracts which you have made; and to be firm and patient in pain (or suffering) and adversity, and throughout all periods of panic. Such are the people of truth, the God-fearing (Qur'an 2:177; similar messages of righteousness are found in Qur'an 4:6, 4:36).

Turning east or west probably refers to the direction one faces while praying. This was established through Divine guidance to be toward the Ka'bah in Mecca (Qur'an 2:144)–a change from the initial direction that Muhammad* chose to face: toward Jerusalem (Abu Dawood 507).

What actions are included among righteous activities?
Doing good to others is more "righteous" than empty rituals.

> Hadeeth: (1) Keeping watch for a day and a night [against enemies] is better than fasting for a whole month and standing in prayer every night (Muslim 4703). (2) God does not need the fasting of those who do not give up evil actions (Bukhari 3.127). (3) The person who looks after a widow or a poor person is like a warrior who fights for God's cause, or like him who performs prayers all the night and fasts all the day (Bukhari 7.265). (4) What a believer continues to receive (in reward) after his death is the righteous deeds he or she performed in this life (Tirmidhi 254).

> Hadeeth: Muhammad* said: The poor [person] of my community would be he who would come on the Day of Resurrection with [lots of] prayers, fasts, and zakah, but since he hurled abuses upon others, brought calumny against others, unlawfully consumed the wealth of others, shed the blood of others, and beat others, his virtues would be credited to the account of those (who suffered at his hand) (Muslim 6251).

Here is a partial list of righteous actions which the Qur'an <u>requires</u> Muslims to follow, arranged alphabetically. The Qur'anic verses cited appear within parentheses. Because similar messages may also occur elsewhere, these verses should be taken as illustrative only. This listing is followed by a listing of undesirable deeds to avoid.

A. Partial list of good practices to follow ("Do's")

<u>Arguments</u>: Present your arguments with beautiful preaching (16:125).

<u>Bequests</u>: Individuals should prepare their wills and bequests (2:180).

<u>Charity</u>: Practice charity regularly (2:43). Kind words are better than charity followed by insult (2:262-4).

    Who should give? Believing men and women (9:71).

    What to give? Only what you have earned honorably (2:267).

    How much to give? What you don't need (2:219); whatever you can (2:215).

    When to give? Regularly (22:78).

    Reward from God: God will double your "credit" (2:261-262).

    Unwilling givers: Charity doesn't count (9:53-9).

    Punishment for not giving: Earning God's displeasure (41:6-7).

    Humility in giving: Be humble; it is better to conceal acts of charity (2:270-271).

    Oaths against giving: Do not take oaths against helping others (24:22).

<u>Cleanliness</u>: Keep your bodies (and environment) clean (4:43; 5:6).

<u>Community</u>: Live a life of righteousness, balance, and moderation (2:143).

<u>Communication</u>: Communicate only good things; do not broadcast evil deeds in public, except to correct injustice (4:148).

<u>Democracy</u>: Conduct your affairs by mutual consultation (42:38).

<u>Discipline</u>: Always be disciplined: follow instructions (58:11).

<u>Divorce</u>: See Chapter 8.

<u>Dress code</u>: See Chapter 7.

<u>Equality</u>: Treat all human beings equally; the only gradation before God is in our degree of righteousness (49:13).

<u>Financial contracts</u>: All contracts should be entered into honestly.

    For on-the spot trade: There is no need for a written contract

(2:282). For transactions involving future obligations: Contracts should be in writing and should preferably be witnessed by either two males, or one male and two females (2:282).

Food: Enjoy all food honestly gotten. Do not eat carrion meat, blood, flesh of swine, and that food on which the name of any other being, other than God, has been invoked. But even these may become acceptable in cases of necessity (2:172-3).

Forgiveness: Seek God's forgiveness for your excesses (57:21); the righteous always forgives (42.37); forgiving is better than retaliation (5:45).

Friendship: The best friends to have are God, His apostle, and other believers (5:55-6).

Good deeds: Do good deeds at all times and to all people (4:36).

Greetings: Respond to a greeting with an even more courteous greeting (4:86).

Honesty: Be honest and speak with honesty and justice (6:151-2); fulfill all fiduciary responsibilities (6:152) and obligations (5:1); and help in righteousness (5:2).

Humility: Always show humility; do not walk on the earth with insolence (17:37).

Inheritance: (a) Before death: People should prepare a will to transfer their estate to others (according to their own wish) (2:180) [and may even give the entire estate to their daughters]. (b) After death [if no will has been made]: There is a prescribed share for relatives (4:11-12). Property of orphans and those of weak understanding should be taken care of honestly (4:5). People should not covet what God has bestowed on others (4:32). Women should not be inherited (i.e., raped, married, etc.) against their will (4:19).

Jihad: Strive in the cause of justice and righteousness (including against base self) (9:20); seek knowledge; help remove misunderstanding; strive for self-improvement (such as giving up smoking and losing weight). Jihad also includes "a defensive struggle" against those who oppress one for one's religion [but an aggressive "holy war" cannot be called Jihad].

Justice/Judgment: Judge with justice (4:58); speak with justice (6:152); trade with justice (6:152).

Kindness: Be kind always, especially to wives, parents, and orphans (2:83, 2:229, 4:5, 17.28, 29.8, 46.15).

Knowledge: Always seek knowledge; travel through the earth to seek the truth (29:20).

Loan repayment: Give debtors time to repay their debts (2:280).

Marriage: See Chapter 8.

Obligations: Fulfill all your obligations with honesty (5:1). Well-off guardians should not take any remunerations for their service (4:6). Do not transfer property to the feeble-minded, but take good care of them (4:5).

Parents: Always treat parents with love, respect, and care (2.83, 17.23-4, 29.8).

Patience: God is with those who persevere patiently (2:153).

People of the Book: Intermarrying with the "People of the Book" is lawful; their food is also lawful (5:5). [Note: Who are "People of the Book"? I believe these include followers of all religions which preach the Oneness of God, which enjoin followers to lead righteous lives, and whose prophets were given a book by God].

Preaching: Invite others to join the Way of God with beautiful preaching; present your points graciously, and listen to their arguments with sincerity (16:125-6).

Protection: Grant asylum to those pagans who seek asylum (9:6).

Punishment: Follow the law equitably, but it is better to forgive (5:45)

Repentance: Seek God's forgiveness earnestly (3:133).

Reward and punishment: Good deeds are rewarded many times over (24:38).

Righteousness: The only ranking before God is in our degree of righteousness (49:13). God loves those who do good (31:17-22). Help in righteousness; not in sin and rancor (5:2).

Trusts: Discharge trusts fully (2:283).

Wills and bequests: Individuals should prepare these before death (2:180).

Witnesses: Be a witness to good deeds; do not witness falsehood (25:72). Number of witnesses needed for financial transactions involving future obligations: Two men, or one man and two women

(2:282-3). Witnesses needed to find anyone guilty of illegal sexual intercourse: Four (24:4).

Here is a partial list of "bad practices" to avoid ("Don't's")

Anger: Do not show anger; pardon others (3:134).

Arguments: Do not dispute with the People of the Book (29:46); do not pursue idle curiosity; avoid empty discourse (6:68).

Arrogance: Do not walk on earth with insolence (17:37; 25:63); do not make fun of others (49:11); God does not love vain behavior (57:23); do not chide those who seek your help (93:10).

Backbiting: Woe to scandalmongers and backbiters (104:1).

Crime: God does not love those who commit crime; all those who do evil harm their own souls (4:107-8).

Deeds: Avoid shameful deeds (53:32).

Discord: Shun those who sow discord (41:36).

Dishonesty: Woe to those who deal in fraud (83:1).

Entering houses: Do not enter others' houses without permission (24:27-9); Enter through the proper door (2:189), and greet each (24:61) Private quarters: Ask permission to enter at times when residents are likely to have night clothes on (24:58-9).

Environment: Do not be wasteful through excess (6:141); God does not love wasteful people (7:31).

Envy: Do not be envious of things that God has bestowed upon others (20:131).

Extravagance: Be neither extravagant nor miserly (25:67).

Falsehood: Do not witness falsehoods (25:72-76).

Fighting: Do not sow discord (41:36); fighting is permitted only to overcome oppression (2:190-3).

Fraud: Woe to those who deal in fraud (83:1).

Gambling: Do not indulge in gambling and other games of chance (2:219).

Insolence: Do not be insolent (17:37).

Intoxicants: These cause more harm than good; therefore, refrain from them (2:219).

Killing: Do not kill anyone except by way of justice (e.g., for committing murder) (6:151). Punishment for wrongful killing: Life for life, but it is better to forgive (2:178) Killing one is like killing many (5:32). Do not kill your children on the plea of want (6:151). Killing of believers is forbidden (4:92-93). Conditions for killing nonbelieiver: Only those who fight you; slay them only to end unprovoked threats to your life; do not transgress limits. If they want peace, you have no reason to fight (2:190-3).

Maligning others: It is sinful to malign others (33:58).

Miserliness: Adopt moderation: be neither miserly nor a spendthrift 17:29).

Oppression: Do not commit oppression, and fight oppression by others in order to end it (2:190-3).

Rumormongers: Woe to rumormongers (104:1).

Suspicion: Avoid suspicion and spying on each other (49:12).

Treachery: Don't be treacherous; but it is permissible to break a treaty with unbelievers if they are treacherous (8:58).

Usury: Do not indulge in usury, doubled and multiplied (3:130). God will deprive usurers of blessing (2:278-279). Give debtors time to repay debts (2:280). [Note: What constitutes usury, however, is not defined].

Violence: Fight only those who fight you, to remove lawlessness and oppression (2:190-3).

Wine and other intoxicants: These cause more harm than good; therefore, refrain from them (2:219).

I didn't know that such a listing even existed in the Qur'an. All that I ever hear is the "Five Pillars of Islam." Why is this so?
The above listing is from the Qur'an, the Divine Book; the emphasis on the "five pillars," discussed below, is from only one Hadeeth.

Are righteous deeds also mentioned in Hadeeth?

> Hadeeth (Righteous activities to adopt): You should like for others what you like for yourself and dislike for others what you dislike for yourself (Tirmidhi 48). Even random acts of kindness, such as removing thorns from people's paths, are liked by God (Bukhari 3.652).

Hadeeth: (Unrighteous activities to avoid): Do not oppress anyone. If you do, seek forgiveness before you die. Else, their sins will be loaded onto you (Bukhari 3.629). Be afraid of the curse of people you oppress (Bukhari 3.626). Avoid suspicion. Do not spy on others. Do not compete with each other, hate each other, or shun each other (Al-Muwatta 47.15). Do not commit robbery (Bukhari 3.654). A person is not a believer when he or she commits any crime (Bukhari 3.655, 7.484, 8.800B, 8.801, 8.763, 8.773).

What righteous deeds are mentioned in the Bible?
Many. Here are the Ten Commandments and the Golden Rule:

Hebrew Scriptures/Old Testament: Ten Commandments (summarized from Exodus 20:3-17):
(1)You shall have no other gods besides Me. (2) You shall not make for yourself a sculptured image, or any likeness of what is in the heavens above or on earth below, or in the waters under the earth. (3) You shall not swear falsely by the name of the Lord your God. (4) Remember the Sabbath day, to keep it holy. (5) Honor your father and your mother. (6) You shall not murder. (7) You shall not commit adultery. (8) You shall not steal. (9) You shall not bear false witness against your neighbor. (10) You shall not covet your neighbor's house: you shall not covet your neighbor's wife, or his male or female slave, or his ox or his ass, or anything that is your neighbor's.
(Rabbi Magid's note: Actually, Jews have 613 commandments. Maimonides, who lived under Muslim rule in Spain and Egypt (1135-1203 CE), divides the 613 into 248 positive commandments ("thou shalts") and 365 negative commandments ("thou shalt nots").

New Testament: You shall love the Lord your God with all your heart, with all your soul, and with all your mind. This is the first and great commandment. And the second is like unto it, You shall love your neighbor like yourself. On these two commandments hang all the law and all the prophets (Matthew 22:37-40. Similar passage: Mark 12:28-34; Luke 10:25-37. The latter includes the story of the Good Samaritan which Jesus used to describe what "loving your neighbor like yourself" meant in practice). Do unto others as you would have them do unto you (Luke 6:31; Matthew 7:12).

ZAKAH (CHARITY)

Zakah (plural: Zakat) may be looked upon as an Islamic "social security tax" that the rich should pay voluntarily to help their financially less fortunate brothers and sisters. In its broader meaning, Zakah includes all virtuous acts which help cleanse out our sins and purify our souls.

Qur'an: Believe in God and His Apostle and spend (in charity) out of the (substance) whereof He has made you heirs. For those of you who believe and spend (in charity), for them is a great Reward (Qur'an 57:7). And whatever you spend in charity or devotion, be sure God knows it all (Qur'an 2:270). Kind words and the covering of faults are better than charity followed by injury (Qur'an 2:263). If you disclose (acts of) charity, even so it is well; but if you conceal them and make them reach those (really) in need, that is best for you: it will remove from you some of your (stains of) evil (Qur'an 2:271).

Hadeeth: Muhammad* explained that it is better to spend your surplus wealth in charity, starting with your own dependents (Muslim 2256); that giving a dirham in charity during one's lifetime is better than giving one hundred dirhams at the moment of his death (Abu Dawood 2860); and that God does not accept charity from goods acquired by embezzlement, just as He does not accept prayer without purification (Abu Dawood 59).

II. DUTIES TO SELF

And what duties to self are Muslims required to fulfill?
Muslims are required to engage in self-development through meditation and the rituals of prayers, fasting, and pilgrimage.

(1) DUTY/RITUAL: SALAT (praying five times a day)

> Qur'an: Recite what is sent of the Book by inspiration to you and establish regular prayer: for prayer restrains from shameful and unjust deeds; and remembrance of God is the greatest (thing in life) without doubt (Qur'an 29:45).

Muslims are to pray five times daily, facing the Ka'bah (Qur'an 2:144). These prayers are: Dawn (fajr), early afternoon (dhuhr), early evening (athar), sunset (maghreb), and night (isha). Congregational prayers are held in mosques on Fridays, at dhuhr time. While there are some rituals for ablution (purification) and prayers, prayers can be shortened if needed. Prayers can even be recited in the heart, and without ablution, if one is traveling. Menstruating and nursing women, and the sick, are exempted from offering ritual prayers. Personal petitionary prayer (du'a) can be offered at any time and in any condition.

> Hadeeth: Many Hadeeth enjoin Muslims to offer prayers (for example, Tirmidhi 571). Others emphasize flexibility in: (a) the number of prayers to be offered daily (Abu Dawood 428); (b) prayer venue and timing in bad weather (Bukhari 1.605 and 1.602); and (c) offering prayers with or without shoes (Bukhari 7.741). Other Hadeeth clarify that (a) Congregational prayers are to be offered in mosques; (b) women can pray in the mosque, even at night (Bukhari 2.22, Bukhari 2.23; Muslim 3217; Abu Dawood 565; Al-Muwatta 14.12); and (c) men

should let women leave the mosque before they do (Bukhari 1.799, 1.825).

Are women required to pray separately or behind men?
No such requirement is found in the Qur'an or Hadeeth. And while some mosques follow a policy of segregation, rows for men and women are adjacent to each other at the Ka'bah in Mecca and in the prophet's mosque in Medina (Islam's holiest places), separated by a path (at the Ka'bah) or a small partition (Medina). Aisha and other women used to pray along with men (Bukhari 1.76, Muslim 7028).

Menstruating women are exempt from offering prayers. But does menstruation make them "unclean" to touch?
No. That is in the Hebrew Scriptures/Old Testament as well as in the cultures of many other groups:

> The Hebrew Scriptures/Old Testament: When a woman has her discharge, her discharge being blood from her body, she shall remain in her impurity for seven days; whoever touches her shall be unclean until evening. Anything she lies on during her impurity shall be unclean; and anything that she sits on shall be unclean. Anyone that touches her bedding shall wash his clothes, bathe in water, and remain unclean until evening; and anyone that touches any object on which she has sat shall wash his clothes, bathe in water, and remain unclean until evening. Be it the bedding or be it the object on which she has sat, on touching it he shall be unclean until evening. And if a man lies with her, her impurity is communicated to him; he shall be unclean seven days, and any bedding on which he lies shall become unclean (Leviticus 15:19-24).

> Qur'an: (Women's courses) are a discomfort and an uncleanliness. Therefore, keep away from women in their courses. And do not approach them (sexually) until they are clean (Qur'an 2:222).

(Regina Pfeiffer's note: The Qur'an passage seems to imply women are "unclean" in the ending part of that passage, "until they are clean.")

Several Hadeeth clarify that there is no stigma in menstruation:

Hadeeth: Aisha (prophet's wife) reported: The prophet used to lean on my lap and recite Qur'an while I was in menses (Bukhari 1.296). Muhammad* once asked Aisha to fetch him the prayer mat from the mosque. She replied: "I am menstruating." He responded: "Your menstruation is not in your hand (Muslim 587). Maimuna (another wife of the prophet) said, "Allah's Apostle was praying while I was in my menses, sitting beside him and sometimes his clothes would touch me during his prostration" (Bukhari 1.376).

The call for prayers sounds spiritually uplifting when one hears it from a distance at dawn; however, it sounds anything but uplifting when many mosques give the same call full blast through loudspeakers. Is this how the adhan is to be made?
No. Adhan is to invite people for prayers in a gentle way and remind us to thank God for all His blessings. Neither are prayers to be recited loudly nor in low tone (Qur'an 17:110). The prophet stressed that people leading prayer should not prolong it in consideration of the sick, the old, and the needy (Bukhari 1.90, 8.13, 9.273).

☛ Ijtihad: Should the use of loudspeakers for adhan be allowed near hospitals and in dense residential areas where there might be many unwell people?

Can prayers be offered anywhere?
God is omnipresent. He is not confined to mosques. Thus, it should be acceptable to offer prayers in most places, except " . . . on a dung hill, in a slaughterhouse, in the middle of the road, in a bathroom, in watering

places for animals, upon the roof of the House of God, and in a graveyard" (Tirmidhi 738).

Is it justifiable to build mosques on paths or roads? Is it true that once a mosque is built, it cannot be torn down?
I believe the answer both questions is no.

☛ Ijtihad: Should mosques be built on disputed land? Should they cause inconvenience to others? Shouldn't it be possible to shift a mosque to a better location if necessary or desirable?

(2) DUTY/RITUAL: SAUM (fasting during the month of Ramadan)

> Qur'an: Fasting is prescribed to you as it was prescribed to those before you, (so) that you may (learn) self-restraint. (Fast) for a fixed number of days; but if any of you is ill or on a journey, the prescribed number (should be made up) from days later (Qur'an 2:183).

Muslims are to fast from dawn to sunset daily during the entire month of Ramadan (29 or 30 days, depending upon the appearance of the moon). Neither can they eat nor drink anything–not even water–nor are they to engage in sex during the fasting hours. Muslims celebrate the end of Ramadan by prayers and charity. This festive day is called the Eid-ul-Fitr (feast of breaking the fast). The other main Muslim religious festival is Eid-ul-Adha (see Haj, below).

In many Muslim countries, no one can eat or drink outside of the house during Ramadan, not even non-Muslims. Doesn't this contradict the injunction, "Let there be no compulsions in religion?"
Yes. There seems to be contradiction here. Nothing in the Qur'an or Hadeeth suggests this level of intolerance. Fasting is supposed to be a soul-purifying and body-cleansing experience; it is also to inculcate discipline, compassion, and piety among us. Seeing others eat and drink should not affect our fasting. After all, Muslims in "non-Muslim" countries fast while others around them are carrying on life as usual.

Hadeeth: Neither should those fasting criticize those not fasting, nor should those not fasting criticize those fasting (Bukhari 3.168, Al-Muwatta 18.23; also, Bukhari 5.575). Those who fast get extra blessings when others around them eat (Tirmidhi 1271, 2081). And those not fasting are rewarded when they serve those fasting (Bukhari 4.140). There is also flexibility regarding when to break the fast in emergencies (Muslim 2486; Al Muwatta 18.21; Bukhari 5.574). (Similar flexibility is found in Bukhari 3.162, 3.176, 3.177, 7.218). The prophet advised people should not fast while traveling (Bukhari 3.167).

Muhammad* advised: If you are invited (for a meal), you should accept it. If you are fasting, you should pray (to bless the inmates of the house). If you are not fasting, you should eat (Muslim 3348).

Breaking fast is no taboo: Once his wives Aisha and Hafsa told Muhammad* that they broke their fast because some food was presented to them. He responded: "There is no harm; keep the fast another day in lieu of it" (Abu Dawood 2451). Once when Muhammad* visited his wife Juwairiya, and learned that she was fasting, he asked her, "Did you fast yesterday?" She said, "No." He said, "Do you intend to fast tomorrow?" She said, "No." He said, "Then break your fast" (Bukhari 3.207).

Embracing and kissing wife during fasting: (Aisha narrates): The prophet used to kiss and embrace (his wives) while he was fasting. (Bukhari 1.319, 3.149, 3.150, 3.151; Abu Dawood 2378, 2380; Muslim 2448; Al Muwatta 17.20, 18.6, 18.14, 18.15).

☛Ijtihad: Is it "Islamic" to prohibit others from eating while we fast? Isn't righteousness more important than our emphasis on how we dress (especially women), how we pray and fast, and how we go about showing others how "religious" we are? Isn't the purpose of prayers and fasting to purify ourselves? Aren't good manners and doing one's duty more important than empty fasts and prayers?

> Hadeeth: The prophet said: "Keeping watch [against enemies] for a day and night is better (in point of reward) than fasting for a whole month and standing in prayer every night" (Muslim 4703), and added that God does not need the fasting of a person who "does not give up . . . evil actions (Bukhari 3.127). He also explained that a person who spends a lot of time in prayers, fasting, and charity–but annoys his neighbor–"will go to Hell." In contrast, another person who engages in fasting, prayers, and charity to a small extent only–but does not annoy the neighbors–"will go Paradise" (Ahmad and Bayhaqi, in Shu'ab al-Iman, 4992).

The end of Ramadan is celebrated with Eid-ul-Fitr. However, often there is disagreement regarding when this should take place. Why?
Since Muslim religious events are based on the lunar calendar, there is usually uncertainty about when events should occur. For example, some insist that the new moon should be sighted in their community or city before the end of Ramadan can be announced. Others feel that, if the new moon is sighted anywhere in the country, it should be acceptable. Thus, in some years, Eid is celebrated on two days.

☞ Ijtihad: Since all heavenly bodies move in space in fixed orbits (Qur'an 21:33), shouldn't we let our scientists determine what should be the "minimum" size of the new moon before it becomes visible at "the first point" on earth? Wouldn't it be nice if the entire world celebrated Eid within a 24-hour period? Is God going to reward me more if I offer my Eid prayers on the "right" day and punish me if I do so on the "wrong" day? Is it more important to show rigidity –and sow discord–or show flexibility–and foster unity?

If fasting hours are to be from dawn to dusk, how can we have Muslims among Eskimos, Lapps (Sammi people), and other people living in extreme latitudes, where a "day" can be up to six months long?

☞ Ijtihad: Shouldn't we follow the Qur'an in spirit rather than letter? Couldn't Muslims living in these extreme latitudes observe the fast for either twelve hours daily or follow the prevailing fasting time in Mecca? Can we also not use the same concept for the daily prayers?

(3) DUTY/RITUAL: HAJ (Pilgrimage to Mecca)

Muslims are to undertake pilgrimage to Mecca at least once in their lifetime if they are physically and financially able to do so. Drawing more than two million pilgrims annually, the Haj is probably the biggest location-specific annual gathering of any kind in the world.

> Qur'an: The first House (of worship) appointed for men was that at Bakka. In it are signs manifest; (for example) the Station of Abraham. Whoever enters it, attains security. Pilgrimage thereto is a duty men owe to God; those who can afford the journey. (Qur'an 3:96-97). Note: Bakka is the old name for Mecca.

Which Abraham's son was to be sacrificed? Ishmael or Isaac?
The Qur'an is unequivocal and clear as to who was to be sacrificed: Ishmael*. The Hebrew Scriptures/Old Testament is neither. According to Genesis 22:1-2, God told Abraham, "Take your son, your only son Isaac, whom you love and offer him as a burnt offering." This statement has an internal contradiction: If God told Abraham* to offer his only son, it could only have been Ishmael*, the first born, and could only have been before Isaac* was born.

☞ Ijtihad: Why should we quibble regarding who was to be sacrificed? Weren't both respected prophets in their own rights? And don't Muslims offer salutations to both in their prayers?

According to the Bible, Abraham lived in Palestine. So how could Hagar have traveled alone with her infant son Ishmael 600-700 miles to Mecca after they were sent away by Abraham?
This puzzle may probably have been solved recently: Based on a study of place-names in Saudi Arabia, Prof. Kamal Salibi suggests that Biblical events prior to around 5th Century B.C.E. took place in the Asir area of Arabia–and not in Palestine (Salibi, 1985).

☞ Ijtihad: Since no evidence of a Jewish presence in Palestine prior to about 5th Century B.C.E. has been uncovered yet, shouldn't the Saudi government permit archeological excavations in the area suggested by Salibi?

THE "FIVE PILLARS OF ISLAM"

What are the "Five Pillars of Islam?"
The article of faith (belief in God), three rituals (prayers, fasting, pilgrimage to Mecca), and charity are usually grouped together as the Five Pillars of Islam, implying that it is incumbent upon Muslims to follow all of them.

If it is "incumbent" upon Muslims to follow the "Five Pillars," what about honesty, hard work, and discipline?
Your observation is valid. While Belief in One God is the basic Article of Faith for Muslims, and prayers, fasting, pilgrimage, and charity are among the essentials of the religion, these five are not grouped together anywhere in the Qur'an or Hadeeth and categorized as the "Five Pillars of Islam"–even once. This categorization conveys the erroneous impression that other righteous deeds such as honesty, discipline, and hard work may be less important. In the Qur'an, these five duties/rituals are so intimately intertwined with other righteous activities that one cannot have belief in God without striving for righteousness. I found only one Hadeeth in which are these five actions listed as "five principles" (Bukhari 1:7). As we saw above in the listing of duties to fellow humans, there are many righteous actions that Muslims are required to follow and

many unrighteous actions they are <u>required</u> to avoid. Thus, merely paying lip service to these "five pillars" without acting on this list of "do's" and "don't's"would make, in my view, a mockery of the religion.

> Hadeeth: (1) Muhammad* clarified that on the Day of Judgment, "poor" Muslims would be those who have performed lots of prayers, fasting, and zakah–but who abused others, unlawfully consumed the wealth of others, and killed others (Muslim 6251). He added that many people who fast obtain nothing from their fasting but thirst, and many who pray obtain nothing but wakefulness. (Tirmidhi 2014).

But, didn't the prophet mention all these five actions in his farewell sermon for Muslims to follow?
Reproduced below is the full text of the prophet's farewell sermon:

(1) "O people, lend me an attentive ear, for I don't know whether, after this year, I shall ever be among you again. Therefore listen carefully to what I am saying, take these words to those who could not be present here today. (2) O people, just as you regard this month, this day, this city as sacred, so regard the life and property of every Muslim as a sacred trust. Return the goods entrusted to you to their rightful owners. Hurt no one so that no one may hurt you. Remember that you will indeed meet your Lord, and that He will indeed reckon your deeds. God has forbidden you to take usury (interest), therefore all interest obligation shall henceforth be waived. (3) Beware of Satan, for the safety of your religion. He has lost all hope that he will ever be able to lead you astray in big things, so beware of following him in small things. (4) O people, it is true that you have certain rights with regard to your women, but they also have rights over you. If they abide by your right, then to them belongs the right to be fed and clothed in kindness. Do treat your women well and be kind to them for they are your partners and committed helpers. And it is your right that they do not make friends with any of whom you do not approve, as well as never commit adultery. (5) O people, listen to me in earnest, worship God, say your five daily prayers,

fast during the month of Ramadan, and give your wealth in Zakat. Perform Hajj if you can afford to. You know that every Muslim is the brother of another Muslim. You are all equal. Nobody has superiority over another except by piety and good action. (6) Remember, one day you will appear before God and answer for your deeds. So beware, do not stray from the path of righteousness after I am gone. (7) O people, no prophet or apostle will come after me and no new faith will be born. Reason well, therefore, O people, and understand my words which I convey to you. I leave behind me two things: the Qur'an and my examples, the Sunnah. f you follow these, you will never go astray. (8). All those who listen to me shall pass on my words to others and those to others again; and may the last ones understand my words better than those who listen to me directly. Be my witness, O God, that I have conveyed your message to your people" (Alim, 1986).

☞Ijtihad: While belief, prayers, fasting, charity, and pilgrimage are mentioned under point 5, doesn't the remaining message, especially points 2, 4, and 6, emphasize righteous actions? Those mentioned include (a) Do not kill or hurt anyone; (b) Do not enrich yourselves by illegal means [i.e., no stealing, bribing, usurping, nepotism, etc.], (c) Do not abuse women, (d) Do not commit adultery, (e) Do not indulge in usury; and (f) Show piety and humility. And under point 5, doesn't the prophet underscore that the "superiority" of anyone over another can only be measured in terms piety and good actions? If piety and righteousness are "superior" to empty prayers and fasting, shouldn't we then consider belief and righteousness as the "Foundation of Islam," without which the "pillars" would crumble?

Unfortunately, prayers, fasting, and pilgrimage are often projected as the main things needed to be a good Muslim and enter paradise. I have often heard Imams (religious leaders) state categorically at Friday prayers, "Brothers, do anything in life, as long as you offer your prayers." The result? The following incident is illustrative:

Personal note: On a visit to Pakistan some years back, I met a former student who greeted me warmly. He also informed me that he had become very rich, "by the Grace of God". I inquired whether he had a high-paying job. He responded negatively. To my next question, "Then, what is the source of your wealth?" he responded matter-of-factly, "I take bribes." I asked, incredulously, "Doesn't your conscience bother you?" His response, confidently, "Why should it? I always offer my prayers!" He was fasting the day we met–"in thankfulness"–because the previous day he had broken his record of daily bribery intake!

☛ Ijtihad: While prayers are to be offered five times a day, fasting is to be observed 29-30 days a year, and haj is to be performed at least once in a lifetime, are not righteous duties to others to be performed all the while every day–and throughout our lives?

☛ Ijtihad: Thus, if the "self-oriented" acts of worship (prayers, fasting, and pilgrimage) are included among "Pillars of Islam," shouldn't we consider duties to others as the "Foundation of Islam"?

CHAPTER 6. JIHAD AND VIOLENCE

I. JIHAD

Does God command Muslims to kill 'infidels' through jihad?
No. Killing anyone is not permitted–except in self-defense and under special circumstances (see below). As we saw in Chapter 4, Islam is highly tolerant–though some of its followers are not. It is probably the only religion which recognizes that God has sent prophets to all nations, all of whom are to be respected equally. Violent and sexist people are found, unfortunately, in all religions. We should not assume their actions represent the teachings of their respective religions. Else, the decades-long violence between Catholics and Protestants in Northern Ireland, between Hindus and Buddhists in Sri Lanka, between Jews and Christians/Muslims in Palestine, and between Hindus and Muslims in India/Pakistan would reflect poorly on these religions. Wouldn't you agree?

> Qur'an: If anyone kills a person–unless it be (in punishment) for murder or for spreading corruption on earth–it would be as if he had slain all mankind; and if anyone saves a life, it would be as if he saved the life of all mankind (Qur'an 5:32).

Then what is jihad?
Jihad means "to strive in a noble way." This encompasses all human actions for self-improvement and enhancing quality of life. Examples include research, information dissemination, and other proactive and positive actions. Muslims are urged to conduct daily this positive jihad by performing righteous and peaceful deeds such as helping the poor, tending to the sick, protecting the weak, giving in charity, showing humility, rising above selfishness, controlling one's ego, and dispelling falsehood. Jihad also includes self-improvement activities such as a

resolve to reduce weight, give up smoking, and control one's base desires. The struggle of Martin Luther King, Jr. to end racial discrimination and segregation in the USA, that of Nelson Mandela to end apartheid in South Africa, and that of Mother Teresa to help the poor in Calcutta are good examples of jihad. Muhammad* considered seeking knowledge to be superior to passive devotion:

> Hadeeth: The prophet said: "If anyone travels in search of knowledge, God will cause him to travel on one of the roads of Paradise. The angels will lower their wings in pleasure and the inhabitants of the heavens and earth will ask forgiveness for the learned man. The superiority of the learned man over the devout is like that of the moon, on the night when it is full, over the rest of the stars. The learned are the heirs of the prophets, and the prophets leave neither dinar nor dirham, leaving only knowledge, and he who takes it takes an abundant portion (Abu Dawood 3634). ["Dinar" and "dirham" are units of currency].

Jihad also includes taking steps to remove tyranny, misunderstanding, and miscommunication–and also to take up arms in self-defense when attacked by enemies on religious grounds. Thus, the only type of war that would qualify as a jihad would be a "defensive struggle." Even in such cases, peaceful jihad is valued higher: "The best jihad is to speak a word of justice to an oppressive ruler" (Dawood 4330).

Doesn't jihad mean "holy war"?
No. The term "holy war" was probably coined by European Christians to describe their crusades in the 11th to 13th centuries, to recover the Holy Land from the Muslims. Sanctioned by the pope, the eight crusades that took place between 1095 and 1272 C.E. caused much human suffering to everyone. They did not result in any long-term gain for the Europeans. The term "crusade" is derived from the Latin "crux" and refers to the Cross of the Crucifixion.

Under what circumstances does the Qur'an permit jihad as a "defensive struggle"?
Only in self-defense and only to counter oppression.

> Qur'an: Fight in the cause of God those who fight you, but do not transgress limits; for God does not love transgressors. . . . And fight them on until there is no more oppression and there prevail justice and faith in God; but if they cease (fighting), let there be no hostility except against those who practice oppression (Qur'an 2:190-193). If the enemy inclines toward peace, you (also) [should] incline toward peace (Qur'an 8:61).

☞ Ijtihad Who should be authorized to issue a call for jihad? Against whom? What should be specific pre-conditions? How do we prevent individuals having their own hidden agenda from issuing such a call? How do we protect the innocent?

Hasn't God promised paradise to those who die in jihad?
God has promised paradise to those who engage in peaceful righteous activities daily as well as to those who lay down their lives defending their religion against oppression and injustice. Peaceful jihad carries a high status; violence is permitted only in self-defense.

What does the Bible say about fighting people of other faiths?
While there are passages of love and compassion in all three books, passages of intolerance and violence also exist in the Hebrew Scriptures/Old Testament. The following are illustrative:

> Hebrew Scriptures/Old Testament: (The Lord said): "Now go attack Amalek, and proscribe all that belongs to him. Spare no one, but kill alike men and women, infants and sucklings, oxen, and sheep, camels and asses!" (1 Samuel 15: 3). And the Lord spoke to Moses: "When you cross the Jordan into the land of

Canaan, you shall dispossess all of the inhabitants of the land; you shall destroy all their figured objects; you shall destroy all their molten images, and you shall demolish all their cult places. And you shall take possession of the land and settle in it, for I have assigned the land to you to possess" (Numbers 33:50-53). "You shall destroy all the peoples that the Lord your God delivers to you, showing them no pity. And you shall not worship their gods, for that would be a snare to you." (Deuteronomy 7:16).

(Rabbi Magid's note: It is important to understand the context of the Amalakites. Despite these verses–and other contradictory ones–the Hebrew Scriptures/Old Testament also makes clear that Jews dwelt with different people in the land, treated them equally, and even married with them. There is a vast difference between text and context.)

(Regina Pfeiffer's note: From a historical-critical perspective, you have cited some of the difficulties with the Hebrew Scriptures/Old Testament, for it does contain these kinds of passages. Yet many of these passages were written or transmitted to show God's faithfulness to people, that God is the One God, and the fulfillment of the promises made to Abraham regarding the land and its occupation. It is a people's experience of what God has done on their behalf).

New Testament: I found no passage asking followers to commit violence.

II. VIOLENCE COMMITTED BY MUSLIMS

Does Islam suggest that Muslims living in non-Muslim countries should try to overthrow the national government by force and establish a "Muslim country"?

No. Muslims are to live in peace and harmony all over the world. Else, how will they fulfill God's commandment: "Invite (all) to the Way of your Lord with wisdom and beautiful preaching; and discuss with them in ways that are best and most gracious" (Qur'an 16:125)? Muhammad* also emphasized:

> Hadeeth: ". . . If you find anything detestable in your rulers, you may hate their administration, but do not withdraw yourselves from their obedience" (Muslim 4573).

☞ Ijtihad: How do we define an "Islamic country?" Shouldn't religious freedom, equality of sexes, social justice, democracy, freedom of speech, and freedom of inquiry be components of this definition? If so, which Muslim countries in the world today can be considered to be "Islamic?"

Wasn't Islam spread primarily by the sword?
True, many Muslims conquered other countries by aggression, which they termed jihad. In their minds, they were not only spreading Islam, but also were enriching themselves. Their actions were probably similar to those of the Conquistadors, who spread Christianity in Latin America through conquest and self-enrichment. However, whether Islam was spread mostly through the sword or through the missionary work of Muslim Sufis or through inter-marrying with people of countries that Muslim travelers and traders visited or settled in, remains unclear. For example, while no Muslim army has ever ventured into Southeast Asia, the world's largest Muslim country, Indonesia, is located there. There also are large Muslim populations in other Southeast Asian countries–and in China and Russia–again where no Muslim army has ever gone.

Then we also have the example of pagan rulers converting to Islam, the religion of the people they conquered: In the 13th Century, the pagan Mongols conquered Baghdad, destroyed its famous library and massacred thousands. Yet within 200 years, the descendants of these pagan rulers embraced Islam and carried back their newly-acquired religion to Mongolia and China.

Were not people forced to convert to Islam or be killed?
In many religions, zealots have been among the worst oppressors. Remember how the Conquistadors spread Christianity in Latin America? Many Muslim rulers probably did likewise. All such cases of religious oppression took place in spite of the message of peace and love found in the Qur'an: "Let there be no compulsion in religion" (Qur'an 2.256).

Doesn't the Qur'an command Muslims to kill apostates–those who convert to Islam but later revert to some other religion?
No. As we saw ib Chapter 4, the Qur'an states: "Those who turn back as apostates after guidance was clearly shown to them: the Evil One has instigated them and buoyed them up with false hopes" (47:25-28).

What do Hadeeth say on the subject?
Here we have a mixed bag: In one Hadeeth Muhammad* forgave apostates for their previous good deeds (Bukhari 9.71-72). But, according to another, he suggested they be killed (Bukhari 9.57).

☛ Ijtihad: Wouldn't killing anyone for becoming an apostate violate the Qur'anic injunction: "Let there be no compulsion in religion" (Qur'an 2:256)? Then could any Hadeeth suggesting death for apostasy be considered true?

Were not the conquered people who did not convert to Islam required to pay some "protection tax?"
The Qur'an instructs that nonbelievers should pay *jizya* (Qur'an 9:29). This tax was probably modeled after the Roman practice of requiring "foreigners" e.g., the Jews, to pay "tribute" tax (Matthew 17: 24-27). In Islam, however the "People of the Book" (especially Jews and Christians) were exempted from paying jizya. In return for paying jizya, the Muslim government accorded non-Muslims full protection and freedom to follow their own belief systems; they were also exempt

from being drafted into the army or from paying other taxes levied on Muslims. In some instances, however, Muslim rulers did not, and currently do not, accord minorities the protection and religious freedom that is guaranteed in the Qur'an.

☛ Ijtihad: Shouldn't all who believe in God, His prophets, His books, His angels, and the Day of Judgment be included among "People of the Book"?

How are "pagans" living in Muslim countries to be treated?
Peace treaties and agreements of mutual help are encouraged. However, if people break these covenants, fighting them is permitted, but only up to a point:

> Qur'an: Do not take for friends hypocrites . . . except those who join a group between whom and you there is a treaty (of peace) or those who approach you with hearts restraining them from fighting you as well as fighting their own people. . . . Therefore if they withdraw from you and do not fight you, and (instead) send you (guarantees of) peace, then, God has opened no way for you (to war against them) (Qur'an 4:89-90).

And how are Jews and Christians to be treated?
As touched upon briefly in Chapter 4, there are three different passages on this subject in the Qur'an, based on time periods involved in the historical development of Islam:

1. In early years, when enemies were trying to crush this fledgling religion, God instructed Muslims to be careful regarding whom they took as friends and trusted with confidential matters:

> Qur'an: Do not take the Jews and Christians for your friends and protectors: they are but friends and protectors to each other" (Qur'an 5:51).

2. Later, as relations improved with the Christian Arabs, the Qur'an's attitude towards them softened. But relations with pagans and Jewish Arabs were still bad. The following verse was revealed after an important battle in which some Jews of Mecca betrayed the Muslims:

> Qur'an: Strongest among men in enmity to the believers will you find the Jews and pagans; and nearest among them in love to the believers will you find those who say, "We are Christians." Because among them there are men devoted to learning and men who have renounced the world, and they are not arrogant (Qur'an 5:82).

3. Finally, after the turbulence that Islam faced initially subsided and things became more settled, God issued some final directives, coinciding with Muhammad's* last days in this world:

> Qur'an: This day are (all) things good and pure made lawful to you. The food of the People of the Book is lawful to you, and yours is lawful to them. (Lawful to you in marriage) are (not only) chaste women who are believers, but (also) chaste women from among the People of the Book. (Qur'an 5:5).

What about other people? Is hostility toward them permitted? Denial of friendship is only for those who fight against Islam:

> Qur'an: God does not forbid you from dealing kindly and justly with those people who do not fight you for (your) faith, nor drive you out of your homes: God only forbids you from turning (for friendship and protection) to those who fight you for (your) faith, drive you out of your homes, and support (others) in driving you out. It is those who turn to them who do wrong (Qur'an 60:8).

Then how do you explain the call for jihad against the West that we hear often from Muslim leaders?
The verse mentioned earlier (Qur'an 60:8) sums up conditions for a military jihad: when the enemy oppresses you, treats you as a second-class citizen, and drives you out of your home. If this continues unabated, then the call for a defensive struggle is justified. While there might be other reasons for going to war (such as the Allies were forced to do in the First and Second World Wars), these should not be called jihad. However, at times leaders call for jihad to accomplish their own personal agenda, disregarding the sufferings this might cause their followers.

☞ Ijtihad Since God requires Muslims to "Invite (all) to the Way of your Lord with wisdom and beautiful preaching; and discuss with them in ways that are best and most gracious" (Qur'an 16:125), shouldn't Muslims spread the message of Islam pro-actively in a peaceful, "mutual learning" mode and by participating in community activities, rather than by adopting a reactive, hostile, and "holier than thou" approach towards "non-believers"?

Why is there so much hatred against America among some Muslims?
This is based primarily on political grounds and has nothing to do with religion. In most cases, it boils down to America's policy in the Middle East. Many Third World people–not just Muslims–feel that the forcible creation of a "homeland" for European Jews in Palestine in 1948, while simultaneously uprooting Palestinian Christians and Muslims from their homeland, was unjustified. Even India's Mahatma Gandhi, born into a Hindu family, was against this creation.

The strong-arm tactics used by America to get the Partition Plan of Palestine passed through the United Nations (Grose, 1982) are considered "economic and military blackmail," by many Third World people. While all people empathized with Jews for the Holocaust, they ask: shouldn't America have carved a homeland for the Jews out of Germany instead? After all, Hitler was responsible for the Holocaust.

Furthermore, Third World people feel, America's ongoing support of Israel by vetoing numerous UN resolutions condemning Israel for its continued occupation of Palestine, its treatment of Palestinians and its illegal settlements in occupied Arab lands only feeds the fire of anti-American feeling in the Middle East and elsewhere. For example, recently 114 countries, including Britain and the rest of the European Union, expressed deep concern about a "deterioration of the humanitarian situation" in Palestinian areas, condemned Jewish settlements there as "illegal" and urged Israel to refrain from "grave breaches" such as "unlawful deportation," "wilful killing," and "torture."Their joint declaration urged Israel to abide by the international laws enshrined in the 1949 Geneva Convention protecting civilians in wartime or under military occupation. While 114 countries voted for this resolution, Israel, USA, and Australia boycotted the session. (Fiona Fleck reporting for the Telegraph, June 12, 2001).

Unfortunately, every such US action, taken with impunity in disregard of global sentiments, is seen by Muslim extremists as a "war against Islam." The result? Muslim radicals gain greater followings. Increasingly they feel the only way to fight the "Great Satan" is through violence, suicide attacks, and destruction. Over the past 50 years, while other problems, such as America's dependence on Middle East oil, have also become undeniably important, the root cause of the problem remains unchanged.

But what about the Jewish dream of a return to Jerusalem after centuries of living in diaspora?
The concept of Zionism (the return of Jews to Palestine) is only about 100 years old. It was authored by Theodor Herzl (1860-1904) in his book *Der Judenstaat* ("The Jewish State," first published in 1896). Herzl urged the establishment of a Jewish homeland in Palestine as an autonomous Jewish commonwealth under the Ottoman Turkish empire. His book outlined the political maneuvering he believed would be necessary to realize this goal. While many European Jews rejected his ideas initially, the Holocaust changed this significantly.

Didn't Yahweh promise Palestine to His Chosen People, the Jews?
Not exclusively, according to the following Biblical passages:

> Hebrew Scriptures/Old Testament: You shall not
> abhor an Edomite, for he is your kinsman. You shall
> not abhor an Egyptian, for you were a stranger in his
> land. Children born to them may be admitted into the
> congregation of the Lord in the third generation
> (Deuteronomy 23:8).
> You shall allot it (the land) as a heritage for yourselves
> and for the strangers who reside among you, who have
> begotten children among you. You shall treat them as
> Israelite citizens; they shall receive allotments along
> with you among the tribes of Israel. You shall give the
> stranger an allotment within the tribe where he
> resides–declares the Lord God (Ezekiel 47:22-23).

☛ Ijtihad (for Jews and Christians): According to the above-
mentioned Biblical passages, doesn't Yahweh's "chosen-ness" now
also extend to the Edomites, Egyptians, and others?

☛ Ijtihad (for Jews and Christians): As Rabbi Avi Magid explains in
Chapter 4, doesn't the concept of "chosen-ness" in general deal with
responsibility, not privilege? Are Zionists fulfilling their responsibility?

☛ Ijtihad: (For Jews and Christians): Didn't Yahweh promise the land
to the children of Israel (for example, Joshua 1:2)? ? Didn't most of
these children convert to Christianity and Islam over the past 2,000
years? And haven't those children continued to live on that land of
their forefather, Abraham*, all the while? So, hasn't Yahweh's
promise been fulfilled all along?

☛ Ijtihad (for Americans): Palestinians ask: Should America's moral
responsibility be to support dogmatically any theocratic ideology
which discriminates against followers of other religions, or should it
be to support morality and justice?

Do all Jews subscribe to the Zionist ideology?
No. Some Jews are opposed to political Zionism. Uri Avnery, a former member of the Israeli Parliament (Knesset), is among them. In his book Israel Without Zionism: A Plea for Peace in the Middle East (1968), Avnery bemoans the futility of Zionism and urges Israel to drop this ideology in favor of peaceful co-existence with the Palestinian Christians and Muslims. His follow-up book, My Friend, My Enemy (1987), describes how the fates of the Israeli people and the Palestinians are intertwined. Another Jewish scholar who questions Zionism is Naom Chomsky, who has written several books on the subject (for example Fateful Triangle: The United States, Israel, and Palestine, 1999).

Is the fight between Israelis and Palestinians a religious war?
No. Palestinians–Christian and Muslim–emphasize their problem is not with Jews, but with "political Zionism," which asserts that Jews from the world over have a right to settle in Israel. While this desire sounds laudable, the problem is that land and water resources are limited. Jewish settlements are expanding by expropriating the land and water of Palestinian Christians and Muslims. While it is nearly impossible for Palestinians to get a permit to build a house, the expansion of Jewish settlements continues unabated, in spite of reservations expressed by America; and while employment opportunities for the Palestinians are limited and jobs in some sectors denied, incoming Jews are given loans and other allowances and provided other incentives.

It appears that whenever a Palestinian is killed, the world (except the USA) condemns Israel. What about killings in other countries?
Loss of lives everywhere should be condemned. However, unlike in most other cases where communal rioting is usually at the "people-to-people" level–which the government tries to quell–the Israeli-Palestinian situation involves a repressed people fighting against the government. And what is beginning to prick American conscience is that situation is the result of our own policies over the past 50+ years.

III. SEPTEMBER 11ᵗʰ TRAGEDY

Can the September 11ᵗʰ tragedy be justified as jihad?
The September 11ᵗʰ tragedy cannot be called jihad. It has been condemned by leaders of all Muslim countries.

Why was this action not condemned by Muslim organizations in America?
All Muslim organizations in America strongly condemned it. Why didn't many Americans learn about this? Perhaps people should ask the media why this news was not prominently disseminated.

Why were some Palestinians shown on TV celebrating this attack?
CNN coverage of some Palestinian youth celebrating September 11ᵗʰ events was a serious "mis-sampling." To be balanced, the coverage should have also shown Palestinian Christians and Muslims praying for the innocent lives which were lost so tragically. But then, the media goes after "newsy" events and not necessarily after accurate sampling. If CNN had gone to gambling casinos in the USA that day, it probably would have found people gambling away, undeterred by the tragedy. Would that have reflected accurately the American mood then?

Parenthetically though, while people the world over shared America's sorrow at this cowardly destruction of life and property, some ask: "Where was America when Israel bombed unarmed civilians incessantly in Beirut in 1982 and then occupied that country through 1985? What about the approximately 20,000 people reportedly killed then (Odeh, 1985)? Was not that attack equally cowardly, probably more so because it was terrorism committed by a state? Why didn't America organize an international coalition to counter that state-sponsored terrorism, a terrorism which continues unabated in the Occupied Territories even today?" In contrast, Muslims increasingly admire European countries for taking a more balanced position on the Israeli-Palestinian conflict, and for providing economic and humanitarian aid with "no strings attached."

Osama bin Laden's call for jihad against the "Christian infidels"
drew thousands to "defend Islam" in Afghanistan; possibly his group
is also training others to continue terrorist attacks. Any comments?
The term "Christian infidel" would be a contradiction of terms and an
insult to the Qur'an as this book includes Christians among "People
of the Book." Undoubtedly, Osama used this phrase to try to rally
extremist Muslims. The Qur'an responds:

> Qur'an: Fear not men but fear Me and sell not My
> Signs for a miserable price. If any do fail to judge by
> (the light of) what God has revealed, they are (no
> better than) unbelievers (Qur'an 5:44).

Secondly, even if Osama attracted 100,000 Muslims (which is also
doubtful), that would account for only one-hundredth of 1% of the
world's Muslim population. People rally to different causes. Let us
recall how European Christians enlisted to join the various Crusades
800 to a 1,000 years ago? Of course many Crusaders were retainers
and servants of the knights–poor people pressed into service whether
they liked it or not. Those Crusades failed badly; Osama bin Laden's
"reverse Crusade" appears to be headed the same way.

Ironically, Osama bin Laden's "Christian and Jewish infidels" also
include scientists who invented the cellular phones, computers, planes,
and airwaves that Osama used and the medicines he took. Isn't it a
hypocrisy that some Muslims want to kill "infidels"–and yet want to
enjoy the fruits of their discoveries? While Muslims scientists led the
world a thousand years ago, in how many areas are they currently at
the cutting edge of research?

Many Muslims are dismayed at this blind hatred. If only Osama had
used his money on Third World development and educating
Americans! Nothing is gained by hatred but much by love, patience,
honesty, and spirituality. Many Americans are supportive of the
Palestinian cause. But acts of violence are turning such people away.

Isn't Yasser Arafat responsible for terrorist attacks by Palestinians?
Shouldn't these be stopped before peace negotiations can resume?
No political leaders has ironclad control over his/her people. Can the U.S. President control the country's Timothy McVeighs and Unabombers? The gripes such Americans have against the government pale compared to the increasing marginalization and economic deprivation the Palestinians are facing at the hands of the Israelis. The situation has deteriorated significantly under the current Israeli Prime Minister Ariel Sharon.

What about the suicide attacks being conducted by the Palestinians?
From the spiritual viewpoint, killing without cause is forbidden in Islam (Qur'an 6:151); this also includes suicide (Qur'an 17:33). The question is: how do you define "just cause"? Here we enter the realm of politics. Remember how the Japanese kamikaze pilots would crash their planes on U.S. ships during World War II? To Palestinians such suicide attacks fall into the same category. The human mind is so powerful that, once determined to achieve a goal, it can do the unthinkable. Abandoned by the world–which itself feels helpless to counter America's unwavering support of Israel in whatever Israel does–the desperate Palestinians feel the only weapon left them is suicide attacks. These young Palestinians are looked upon as martyrs by their people. While we may not support such action, to Palestinian Christians and Muslims, having been driven from their homes and facing increasingly repressive economic and religious discrimination, this is a justifiable jihad. And based on the pattern of voting in the United Nations, the rest of the world continues to support the Palestinian struggle. Isn't this unwavering U.S. support for Israel helping to create the Osama bin Ladens of the world?

This is the opposite of the information our media carries. Where can I learn more about the Palestinian viewpoint?
Read the book written by Naim Ateek (1989), a Palestinian Christian and cannon of St. George's Cathedral in Jerusalem and pastor of its Arabic-speaking congregation. A book discussing the role of media in covering Middle East events was co-edited by Prof. Edward Said, a

Palestinian scholar (1996). The Arab-American Anti-Discrimination Committee (http://www.adc.org/) and the National Council on US-Arab Relations (http://www.ncusar.org/) are active community-based organizations covering the Middle East. Muslim websites include http://www.amconline.org/newamc/ (American Muslim Council) and http://www.isna.net/ (Islamic Society of North America).

What about newspapers and periodicals?
I find the Christian Science Monitor to be objective in its reporting of the Middle East conflict. For example, see John Cooley's analysis (http://www. csmonitor.com/2002/0131/p09s02-coop.html), "Israel's especially cruel sanctions," in the paper's January 31, 2002. Similarly, I find the London Times to be objective. Among periodicals I find the Washington Report on Middle East Affairs (http://www.wrmea.com) to be balanced. Among television networks, I find BBC Middle East coverage to be objective. In contrast, I understand that CNN coverage of world news for the rest of the world is different from its coverage for America. Thus, viewers elsewhere often learn more about the Middle East than viewers in America.

What about official U.S. government reports?
Visit http://usinfo.state.gov/regional/nea/mitchell.htm for the April 30, 2001 report of the Sharm El-Sheikh Fact-Finding Committee. This committee was chaired by former U.S. Senator George J. Mitchell.

Is there any protest among Israeli Jews against the discriminatory treatment of Palestinians by the Israeli government?
Yes. Increasingly Israeli Jews–especially women– being alarmed at the growing number of Israeli casualty in the ongoing conflict and also getting disturbed at the inhuman treatment of Palestinians by the Israeli government, are voicing their protest. An embarrassing blow to the Israeli government was the recent refusal by more than 100 Israeli military reserves to serve in the Occupied Territories. And Rabbi Michael Lerner has started a protest movement against the occupation (www.RabbiLerner@tikkun.org). In this regard, a letter by Ishai

Menuchin, leader of "Israeli Soldiers' Movement for Selective Refusal" appeared in the March 9 2002 issue of the New York Times.

Do people in Muslim countries find anything positive about the USA?
Yes. There is much admiration for America's championing the cause of peace, justice, freedom, and democracy in the world (except in Israel), and the advancements that Americans and Europeans have made in many fields, such as science, technology, and medicine.

But doesn't America justify its firm support to Israel by asserting that it is our only reliable ally in that strategic region?
Yes it does. But at what cost? Palestinian Christians and Muslims point out that while America adopts a firm posture against other allies whenever human rights are violated, the same principles are usually thrown by the wayside whenever it involves Israel. To what extent will America continue to bend over backward to meet Israeli demands and overlook its violence? Even when this violence is committed against Americans and American military personnel are killed by Israelis?

What do you mean? When could have that happened?
Read The Attack on the *USS Liberty* and its Cover-up (Akins, 2000). A former U.S. ambassador to Saudi Arabia, Akins describes how, on June 8, 1967, Israeli warplanes attacked this World War II-vintage American freighter while it was conducting advanced communications research in the eastern Mediterranean Sea, in international waters. Akins narrates:

> "The first attack lasted about five minutes. A few minutes later, three unmarked Super-Mysteres attacked with napalm and dozens of rockets. There was then a short respite, and two more Mirages, also unmarked, attacked. The entire two-part engagement lasted about 22 minutes. Nine men had been killed and about 60 wounded . . . While most of the lifeboats had been destroyed in the first attack, the ship managed to launch three [lifeboats], but they were immediately attacked by

Israeli motor torpedo boats. The Israelis destroyed two of the lifeboats–a war crime in itself–and captured the third. The torpedo boats also fired their cannons into the ship in an apparent last attempt to sink it. The carnage continued until 171 American sailors were wounded, many severely, and 34 were killed.

When the Israelis saw that they were unable to sink the ship after more than two hours of intense attack, they offered support to the survivors. Captain McGonagle, who had been badly wounded himself, refused, and his ship limped into Malta, where 821 rocket and missile holes more than 3,000 holes from armor piercing bullets were counted. In subsequent "explanation," the Israeli said they had mistaken the ship for the Egyptian *"al-Qusair,"* although the ships' profiles had nothing in common: the Egyptian ship displaced 2,000 tons, while the American ship displaced 10,000 tons. The *Liberty* was clearly marked, and it flew a standard American flag that measured five-by-eight-feet. The flag was destroyed during the first attack, but it was replaced immediately by a nine-by-15 foot "holiday flag," which remained aloft throughout the subsequent attacks. The Israelis never attempted to explain how they had acquired the frequencies on which the ship transmitted, and why they had blocked them (the Egyptian frequencies would have been quite different). Nor have they explained why their aircraft were unmarked, or why the American flag was ignored."

How could the American Congress have remained silent on such an uncalled-for attack on an American ship in international waters? And why was this not covered in headlines by our media?
Some people cynically refer to our Congress and media as "Israeli-Occupied Territories."

IV. GROPING FOR A JUST SOLUTION
FOR THE MIDDLE EAST CONFLICT

What must "happen" to bring about a change in U.S. foreign policy?
A change of heart in the U.S. Congress; a change–Palestinians remind
us–which ranks adherence to the principle of *Human Rights and
Justice for All*, enshrined in the U.S. Constitution and Bill of Rights,
above short-term and "self-preserving" tactics of yielding to pressures
from the Zionist lobby.

*These are very strong words! How can these Palestinians prove their
accusations against our lawmakers?*
Read the book They Dare To Speak Out (1991). Written by former
Congressman Paul Findley, this provides unsettling accounts of what
happens to members of the U.S. Congress who try to adopt even a
neutral position vis-a-vis the Israeli-Palestinian conflict. Additionally,
the Washington Report on Middle East Affairs mentioned earlier
(http://www.wrmea.com) keeps readers current on happenings in the
U.S. Congress related to the Middle East, including financial
contributions received by members of the U.S. Congress.

Why don't we learn about this in the popular media?
It is not only what is reported but also how it is reported. For example,
Palestinians bemoan, while the suicide attacks carried out by individuals
are labeled by our press as "carnage" and "bloodbath," the Israeli
attacks employing the mightiest army in the region–supported by
American tax dollars and in which three to four times more people are
killed–are projected as justified retaliatory countermeasures.

What role can the President play?
It is generally lamented that most U.S. Presidents tend to accede to all
the wishes of the pro-Israeli lobby. Palestinians remind us that the only
U. S. President who challenged successfully this lobby over the last
60+ years was Eisenhower. In 1956, when Britain, France, and Israel
collectively invaded Egypt after President Nasser nationalized the Suez
Canal, Eisenhower's firm threat to intervene forced these three

countries to withdraw–unceremoniously. Palestinians feel that so far every other President seems to have succumbed to the Lobby.

What about President George Bush?
He let a great opportunity slip by immediately after 9/11, when he had the entire nation firmly united behind him. That support could have enabled him to withstand any media blitz by the Israeli Lobby and help bring about a just settlement of the Israeli-Palestinian conflict. Palestinians ask: "Do we again have the case of the 'tail wagging the dog'? Or is the US merely the tail?"

What about the recent Saudi proposal suggesting a formal recognition of Israel by Arab countries in return for an Israeli withdrawal to the 1967 borders?
That proposal echoes the United Nations Security Council Resolutions 242 of 1967 and 338 of 1973. Nothing has happened so far on those resolutions, Palestinians remind us, because of Israel's defiance and U.S. reluctance to annoy the Lobby. Can President Bush show the same firmness that Eisenhower demonstrated in 1956?

What about the European Union Russia and other countries?
Because of the veto power enjoyed by the Security Council's five permanent members (Britain, China, France, Russia, and USA), nothing can happen if even one of these members vetoes a resolution. The USA has so far probably vetoed more than 30 resolutions calling for a just settlement of the Middle East conflict–while other Security Council members have voted for those resolutions.

If the situation is so helpless, what can the average American do?
Currently, less than 50% Americans vote. Rather than helping the situation, their inaction only empowers single-issue lobbies to have a field day. The institution of democracy is still the best system on a sustained basis. But it needs people to exercise their rights. It takes 51 Senators to bring about any change in U.S. foreign policy. Voters should learn from the Zionist lobby: they should work to get people elected who are sympathetic to their cause.

The beauty of the American system of checks-and-balances is such that there is little the U.S. president can do without Congressional support. No amount of saber-rattling or threat against "the great Satan," or calling Americans (or Christians) "infidels," will work; on the contrary, these will continue to have the opposite effect. Currently, almost any pro-Israel resolution introduced into Congress–no matter how damaging it might be to America's long-term interests–routinely gets 80% or more of the votes in both Houses of Congress.

Why?
Most of the world will say this is because money talks. Since it takes millions of dollars to run for the U.S. Congress, elected officials are often quite willing to "listen" to what their benefactors may demand. Both of our major political parties, it appears, try to outdo each other in expressing their support for Israel–regardless of what Israel does.

☞ Ijtihad (for Americans): Doesn't our current system of corporate and individual financial contributions to political parties and candidates discriminate against poor Americans? Shouldn't our government consider adopting the system, being successfully used in several European countries, where there is only public financing of elections?

How can our system be changed?
By people's voice. Currently, about 50% of America's registered voters do not vote. Reasons include apathy, frustration, and misgiving. Add to this number those Americans who are eligible to vote but are not yet registered, and we find that most politicians are elected by a minority of people. Thus there is a great opportunity for concerned people to join hands to empower these apathetic people.

What approach would you suggest to American Muslims to adopt to help make the U.S. policy on the Middle East more equitable?
As patriotic citizens, American Muslims should: (1) embrace warmly the American political system and contribute to the country's further development; (2) reach out to those who are not participating currently in the country's democratic process; (3) participate actively in civic,

cultural, and philanthropic activities at the local, state, and national levels; (4) learn about other cultures and values systems; (5) network with other religious and civic groups, specially Jewish groups which are sympathetic to the Palestinian cause; and (6) have patience as needed changes in any democratic system may take many years to be realized.

But what about legitimate Israeli security concerns?
Since the Israeli strategy of insisting on security guarantees before implementing UN Security Council resolutions 242 and 338 and withdrawing from the Occupied Territories has failed, shouldn't it now try the opposite and withdraw from these territories first?

And what approach would you suggest to Muslims worldwide to adopt to help spread the message of Islam positively?
A two-pronged approach is suggested: (1) Extremists should realize that nothing is gained by violence. Apart from the fact that killing innocent people is un-Islamic, it is also an exercise in futility in the current geopolitical context. What did the 9/11 tragedy accomplish? And what is the senseless killing of other innocent non-Muslims in other countries   accomplishing–even if it is "in retaliation" for the killing of innocent Muslims by others? Such violence, even in the pursuit of "just causes," only increases the world's resolve to fight terrorism; it is turning away many friends; and it is making harder the task of pro-Palestinian Americans. (2) The silent majority of Muslims (see Chapters 14 and 15) should become active and follow Qur'anic guidance, beautifully articulated in these and other verses:

> Qur'an: Invite others to the Way of your Lord with wisdom and beautiful peaching; and discuss with them in ways that are best and most gracious (Qur'an 16:125).

> Qur'an: . . . Those who believe and enjoin patience (constancy and self-restraint) and enjoin deeds of kindness and compassion. Such are the Companions of the Right Hand (Qur'an 90:17-18)

CHAPTER 7. STATUS OF WOMEN
AND EFFEMINATE MEN

I. STATUS OF WOMEN

Men in some Muslim societies appear to be sexist and women, repressed. To what extent is this based on the Qur'an?
This is cultural (as defined by men, of course) and does not represent Islamic teachings. This will become clear in this and the following two chapters.

1. General Guidelines

> Qur'an: Men are the protectors and maintainers of women because God has given the one more (strength) than the other and because they support them from their means. Therefore, the righteous women are devoutly obedient, and guard, in (their husband's) absence what God would have them guard. As to those women on whose part you fear disloyalty or ill-conduct, admonish them (first), (next), refuse to share their beds (and last), beat them (lightly). But if they return to obedience, seek not against them means (of annoyance) (Qur'an 4:34).

Doesn't the latter part of this verse assert categorically that husbands are "superior" and that wives are to show them unquestioned obedience?
Yes, this verse appears "sexist." However, the check-and-balance between husband and wife, discussed below and in the next two chapters, will clarify that the wife has much freedom– including the freedom to divorce her husband.

☛ Ijtihad: Doesn't the above-mentioned verse (Qur'an 4:34) require wives to be "devoutly obedient" to their husbands <u>because</u> husbands are the "maintainers and protectors of women"? If so, how should we apply this verse nowadays in situations where the wife becomes the "maintainer" by earning more money than the husband and also the "protector" by being more intelligent than he? Consider:

> Qur'an: It is We who have sent down to you this Book. In it are verses basic or fundamental (of established meaning). They are the foundations of the Book. Others are not of well-established meaning [allegorical]. But those in whose heart is perversity follow the part thereof that is not of established meaning (Qur'an 3:7).

☛ Ijtihad: Shouldn't we take Qur'anic verse 4:34 allegorically–with the bottom line message being that the head of household (whether husband or wife) should be the final decision maker? Wouldn't this be similar to the fact that, while the Qur'an exhorts Muslims to treat slaves kindly and set them free (Chapter 11), that verse would hardly find application nowadays–except that the principle could be applied to all people entrusted to one's command?

Are there passages in the Bible which require wives to be submissive to their husbands?

> New Testament: Wives, submit yourselves unto your husbands, as unto the Lord. For the husband is the head of the wife, even as Christ is the head of the church: and he is the savior of the body. Therefore, as the church is subject unto Christ, so let the wives be to their own husbands in every thing. Husbands, love your wives, even as Christ also loved the church, and gave himself for it. . . . So ought men to love their wives as their own bodies. He that loves his wife loves himself (Ephesians 5:22-28). Wives, submit yourselves unto your own husbands, as it is fit in the Lord. Husbands,

love your wives and be not bitter against them
(Colossians 3:18-19).

But nowadays, while Christians do not necessarily follow such
guidelines dogmatically, many Muslims, it appears, do. Isn't it so?
You are right. However, we should not judge any religion by what
some of its followers do, but only by what the religion's sacred text
stipulates. Some Muslims are sexist, and their actions, I believe, violate
Qur'anic injunctions. Such behavior reflects human weaknesses and
cultural norms rather than religious teachings.

How did Muhammad* treat his wives?
Muhammad* had thirteen wives, of whom only one–Aisha–was
previously unmarried. Others were either divorcees or widows (see
Chapter 8). Apparently there was much love among them all and equal
relationships. In fact, his wives even argued with him occasionally:

> Hadeeth: Once Umar (who later became Caliph No. 2)
> asked his daughter Hafsa (who was one of
> Muhammad's* wives): whether she argued with the
> prophet? When she replied in the affirmative, Umar
> asked Muhammad* if this was true. In response,
> Muhammad* simply smiled (Bukhari 3.648, 6.435).

2 . Behavior and Dress Code

The talk of equality is fine, but what about status? For example, are
not women <u>required</u> to wear the veil–the hijab?
The Qur'an guides men and women to dress and behave modestly:

> Qur'an: Say to the believing men that they should lower
> their gaze and guard their modesty: that will make for
> greater purity for them. And say to the believing
> women that they should lower their gaze and guard
> their modesty; that they should not display their beauty
> and ornaments except what (must ordinarily) appear

> thereof; that they should draw their veils over their
> bosoms and not display their beauty except to their
> husbands, their fathers, . . . and that they should not
> strike their feet in order to draw attention to their
> hidden ornaments (Qur'an 24:30-31).

As we see, the "veil" to be drawn is over her bosoms and not over her
face. And, while in public, the Qur'an asks women, including the
prophet's wives, to wear an "outer garment."

> Qur'an: O prophet! Tell your wives, daughters, and
> (other) believing women that they should cast their
> jilabib (outer garments) over their persons (when
> abroad): that is most convenient that they should be
> known (as such) and not molested (Qur'an 33:59).

How do you define "outer garment"?
The Qur'anic verse 24:31 only stipulates that women "should draw
their veils over their bosoms." Beyond that, there appears to be much
flexibility. Thus nowadays, the "outer garment" varies from head-to-
foot veiling by Saudi women, through blouse and skirt worn by
Bosnian women, to only saree with no blouse worn by some poor
Bangladeshi village women, with the end of their saree covering their
bosoms. Are these Bosnian and Bangladeshi women any "less
religious" than their Saudi counterparts?

But what about the hijab–the total bodily covering--that women are
required to wear in some countries?
No Qur'anic verse requires women to wear any veil, face veil or any
other type. The word "hijab" is mentioned only once in the Qur'an,
and that too only in reference to the prophet's wives:

> Qur'an: O you who believe! Do not enter the prophet's
> houses until leave is given to you for a meal, (and then)
> not (so early) as to wait for its preparation. But when
> you are invited, enter, and when you have taken your

meal, disperse, without seeking familiar talk. Such (behavior) annoys the prophet. He is ashamed to dismiss you, but God is not ashamed (to tell you) the truth. And when you ask (his ladies) for anything you want, ask them from before a screen ("hijab"): that makes for greater purity for your hearts and their hearts. Nor is it right you should annoy God's messenger, or that you should marry any of his widows after him at any time (Qur'an 33:53).

Comparing this with verse 33:59 discussed earlier, we see that, while the instruction for observing the hijab applied only to the prophet's wives and only when people visited the prophet's house, all women (including the prophet's wives) are instructed to wear an "outer garment" in public.

Hadeeth: Umar suggested to Muhammad* that, since good and bad persons visited his house, he should ask his wives to wear veils. The [above-mentioned] verse of hijab [33:53] was then revealed (Bukhari, 6.10, 6.313); similar Hadeeth were also reported by Aisha (Bukhari 1.148, 4.130, 7.166, 7.36, 7.40, 8.177, 8.257). After Muhammad* got married to Zainab, he hung a curtain (hijab) between others and himself (Bukhari, 7.375; also: 6.315, 6.316, 6.317, 7.95, 9.517).

These Hadeeth re-confirm the following: (a) Who were required to observe "hijab"? Only the prophet's wives; (b) When was "hijab" required? When people visited the prophet's house.

The fact that there is no face veiling in Islam is perhaps best observed at the Ka'bah (Chapter 5). There, women are not allowed to cover their faces at all. After all, the intent in one's heart counts a lot: a woman can be completely veiled and appear vulgar; another woman may be in tatters with little clothing and still be modest. Nowadays, in some cultures, hijab is defined as a scarf covering the head and neck. While this "modernization" would probably be criticized as "un-Islamic" by some conservative Muslims, it is considered a welcome change by more liberal Muslims.

Are there any Hadeeth in which women are not veiled?

> Hadeeth: (1) During the Battle of Uhud, Aisha and Umm Salama (prophet's wives) carried water skins on their backs, with their robes tucked up so that their bangles were visible (Bukhari 4.131).
>
> (2) Women helped men in various battles (Muslim, 4456).
>
> (3) The prophet permitted Fatima (his daughter) and other ladies to wear dyed clothes and apply eye make-up (Fiqh as-Sunnah 5.19).
>
> (4) During pilgrimage, a beautiful woman sought the prophet's advice on some matter. A companion of the prophet stared at her. The prophet turned away the companion's face (Bukhari 8.247).
>
> (5) Among female prisoners of war, the prophet saw a woman lifting up children to her [exposed] breasts for nursing. Impressed, he praised and remarked, "God is [even] more merciful to His slaves than this woman is to her sons" (Bukhari, 8.28).
>
> (6) Aisha narrated to Muhammad* the story of a man who was so enamored by seeing the two young sons of a woman play with her breasts that he married her. Muhammad* responded: "I am to you like that man was to that woman" (Bukhari 7.117).

To what degree were these women veiled? In Case (3), the prophet turned his companion's face away from staring at the young woman; but he did not instruct her to put on a veil. Similarly, while Cases (4) and (5) are about women with exposed breasts, the prophet did not comment negatively about this. Obviously their intention was one of nature's most beautiful moments: mother nursing child.

> Hadeeth: If someone intends to do a good deed but does not, God will credit his account with a full good deed. If he actually does the good deed, God will credit his account with ten to seven hundred more times. If someone intends to do a bad deed but does not do it, God will credit him with a full good deed. If he actually does it, then God will write one bad deed in his account (Bukhari 8.498).

☞Ijtihad: Thus, shouldn't the primary consideration in all human actions be the intention of the party undertaking an act?

Then on what basis are many Muslim women are required to be completely covered?
Probably on the basis of the following Hadeeth:

> Hadeeth: Asthma, daughter of Abu Bakar, visited the prophet wearing thin clothes. The prophet said: "O Asthma, when a woman reaches the age of menstruation, it does not suit her to display her parts of body except this and this," and he pointed to her face and hands (Abu Dawood 4092).

Saleem, what are your views on veiling?
The bottom line should be one's intentions:

> Hadeeth: Muhammad* said, "The value of [one's] deeds are determined by [one's] intentions" (Fiqh-us Sunnah 3.10A, Bukhari 1.51, Tirmidhi 5320).

No legislation or threat of hellfire can hide what is in our hearts. A veiled woman can behave in a vulgar manner and a sparsely clothed woman (because of necessity) be very modest. The same applies to men. Women should be free to choose whether they want to wear a veil and what type without societal pressure. And we should not talk ill of women who choose not to wear a veil. Unfortunately, chiding women to wear the veil is the second-most common subject in sermons at Friday prayers– next only to asking men to "do anything in life–as long as you offer prayers."

Personal note: After my parents got married in the mid 1920s (an arranged marriage), my father encouraged my mother, then a high-school graduate, to study further; he also advised her to stop wearing the veil. Coming from a conservative Muslim family where girls accepted veiling happily as the sign of "coming of age," my mother was shocked. For a long time she felt inadequately dressed when she went out in public without her veil; as if her "security blanket" had been snatched away. However, recovering from this initial inhibition, she continued with her education and got Masters degrees in Urdu (my mother tongue) and English. My father died in 1951 (I was then eleven), shortly after we moved from India to Pakistan (following the partition of British India). There, we and many other families were starting life afresh, having left everything behind in India. The same, of course, was also true of Hindus and Sikhs who migrated from Pakistan to India. Fortunately, being educated, my mother got a job as a school teacher. On that meager salary, she sent her four children (two girls and two boys) to college. After graduating, my sisters also worked. So my brother and I were raised on the earnings of three women. How much progress would they have made if they wore a veil? Only God knows.

By gender segregation, I believe we cut the work force in half. While it may be argued that women should stay at home, who will take care of widows (like my mother) and other single women? To what extent can close relatives help? Also, job opportunities for veiled women are generally limited to professions such as teaching, nursing, and dressmaking. What if women want to become engineers, geologists, space technologists–even heads of states?

In some cultures, touching other people, including those of the opposite sex, is very common. For example, Hawaiians greet each other by kissing and embracing, and Eskimos rub noses. Will these be prohibited if they became Muslims?

People should not be stopped from following positive cultural practices. In Hawaii, you honor your guest and show camaraderie by an embrace, an aloha kiss, and a garland ("lei"); among the Eskimos, you rub noses. Having lived in Hawaii for nearly 30 years now, I haven't noticed any adverse effect of the aloha kiss on anyone. On the contrary, people of diverse ethnic backgrounds, such as Japanese, Chinese, Koreans, Filipinos, and Caucasians, who now make Hawaii their home, have also adopted this practice. Thus, warmth and friendship prevail almost everywhere; people are usually always smiling and are very helpful.

Probably it was because of this prevailing fellow-feeling in this tropical paradise that no anti-Muslim incident occurred here following the September 11th tragedy. On the contrary, many people called me and other Muslims to inquire about our safety and show their support. With so much violence the world over, other cultures might want to consider adopting the aloha practice of Hawaii. I imagine the Eskimo practice also has similar effect. The bottom line should be one's intention.

Respect for other cultures is also highlighted in the following Qur'anic narration of how Dhu al Qarnayn, a legendary God-fearing king, "left alone" some people to follow their cultural practice:

> Qur'an: "When Dhu al Qarnayn came to the rising of the sun, he found it rising on a people for whom We had provided no covering protection against the sun. (He left them) as they were: We completely understood what was before him" (Qur'an 18:83-91).

Yusuf Ali (1989) suggests these were primitive people living simple lives. Perhaps the climate was hot, and they required neither roofs over their heads nor much clothing to protect them from the sun.

☛Ijtihad: To what extent should cultural values be swept away by religious dogmas? Should, for example, Bangladeshi women working under hot, humid conditions in rice fields be required to be completely veiled from head to foot like Saudi women, or wear the "chador" like their Iranian sisters, or wear a face mask like their Yemeni sisters–or continue to wear the sari, as they have been doing for centuries? Should Muslims in Hawaii stop greeting visitors with a "lei" (garland) and an aloha kiss? Should Eskimo Muslims not greet each other by rubbing noses?

What do the Hebrew Scriptures/Old Testament and New Testament say about veiling and/or sexism?

> Hebrew Scriptures/Old Testament: (1) Most books were written from a patriarchal perspective.
> (2) "Because the daughters of Zion are so vain and walk with their heads thrown back, with roving eyes and with mincing gaits, making a tinkling with their feet–My Lord will bare the pates of the daughters of Zion, the Lord will uncover their heads. In that day, my Lord will strip off the finery of their anklets, the fillets, and the crescents; of the eardrops, the bracelets, and the veils; the turbans, the armlets, and the sashes; of the talisman and the amulets; the signet rings and the nose rings; of the festive robes, the mantles, and the shawls; the purses, the lace gowns, and the linen vests; and the kerchiefs and the capes. And then–instead of perfume, there shall be rot; and instead of an apron, a rope; instead of a diadem of beaten work, a shorn head; instead of a rich robe, a girding of sackcloth; a burn instead of beauty. Her men shall fall by the sword, her fighting manhood in battle; and her gates shall lament

and mourn, and she shall be emptied, shall sit on the ground"(Isaiah 3:16-26).

(Rabbi Magid's note: This section deals with women's shortcomings/failings as human beings in the context of the men's failings too).

(Regina Pfeiffer's note: Isaiah and other prophets may indicate veils as part of clothing of the woman, but veiling was not prescribed in the sense that women had to cover themselves. Many of the prophets use imagery (Hosea, for example) to express the relationship between God and the community because the community is unfaithful to the covenant. Harlotry was one of those images).

New Testament: (1) "Every man praying or prophesying, having his head covered, dishonors his head. But every woman that prays or prophesies, with her head uncovered, dishonors her head: for that is even all one as if she were shaven. For if a woman not be covered, let her also be shorn; but if it be a shame for a woman to be shorn or shaven, let her be covered. For a man indeed ought not to cover his head, forasmuch as he is the image and glory of God; but the woman is the glory of man. For the man is not of the woman, but the woman is of the man. Neither was the man created for the woman, but the woman for the man"(1 Corinthian 11:4-9).

(2) "I desire, then, that in every place the men should pray, lifting up holy hands without anger or argument; also that the women should dress themselves modestly and decently in suitable clothing, not with their hair braided, or with gold, pearls, or expensive clothes, but with good works, as is proper for women who profess reverence for God. Let a woman learn in silence with full submission. I permit no woman to teach or to have

authority over a man; she is to keep silent" (1 Timothy 2:8-12).

(Regina Pfeiffer's note: Yes, there are many passages that relegate women to subservient roles. But in terms of the manner in which Jesus treated women, which really is the model, and not so much the letters of Paul (and in the ones cited above, deutero-Paul), he (Jesus) treated them with equality and dignity, overcoming some of the biases of his time (for example, the woman with the hemorrhage, Martha and Mary of Bethany, Mary of Magdala, and the Samaritan woman at the well). What is even more important is that a woman was among the first witnesses to the Resurrection at a time when a woman could not be a legal witness).

3. Women as Witnesses

Isn't it true that the testimony of two women equals that of one man? This applies only when dealing with financial transactions involving future obligations:

> Qur'an: "When you deal with each other in transactions involving future obligations in a fixed period of time, reduce them to writing. . . . And get two witnesses out of your own men. If there are not two men, then a man and two women such as you choose for witnesses so that if one of them errs the other can remind her" (Qur'an 2:282).

☛ Ijtihad: Doesn't the initial qualifying clause in verse 2:282 makes it clear that only in matters dealing with financial transactions involving future obligations that one man's testimony equals that of two women–and not in other matters?

☛ Ijtihad: What happens if the man errs? Also, as discussed earlier, how do we apply this verse nowadays when women, even in sexist societies, are turning out to be more intelligent than men? Thus, should we not also take this verse allegorically rather than literally?

What does the Bible say about women as witnesses?
This subject is not discussed directly–although, as Regina Pfeiffer points out in her above-mentioned note, women could not serve as witnesses. And, in many passages, it appears that all witnesses were men (see, for example, Jeremiah 32:12; Ruth 4:9).

4. Status of Women in the Hereafter

How do women "measure up" against men in the Hereafter?
They are equal. Our reward and punishment will depend on our deeds:

> Qur'an: If any do deeds of righteousness–be they male or female–and have Faith, they will enter Heaven, and not the least injustice will be done to them (Qur'an 4:124). God has promised the hypocrites, men and women, and the rejecters of faith, the fire of hell (Qur'an 9:67-68).

However, in contrast, we have the following sexist Hadeeth:

> Hadeeth: (1) The prophet said, ". . . I found the majority of people entering hell were women." (Bukhari 1.28, 2.161, 4.464, 7.124-26, 8.555; Muslim 6597. A similar account is found in Muslim 6600).

☞Ijtihad: Could Muhammad* have said this? Either we conclude that majority of women are inherently "wicked," or we need to reject this Hadeeth outright. It appears to violate the very ethos of the Qur'an.

Wasn't it Eve who caused Adam to sin?
That's in the Hebrew Scriptures/Old Testament and the New Testament; in the Qur'an, both were equally guilty:

> Hebrew Scriptures/Old Testament: The man (Adam) said, "The woman (Eve) You put at my side–she gave me of the tree, and I ate it." (Genesis 3:14)

> New Testament: And Adam was not deceived, but the woman being deceived was in the transgression (1 Timothy 2:14).

> Qur'an: Then did Satan make them (Adam and Eve) slip from the (garden) and get them out of the state (of felicity) in which they had been (Qur'an 2:36).

II. STATUS OF EUNUCHS AND EFFEMINATE MEN

Aren't effeminate men and eunuchs discriminated against?
No. The Qur'an does not discuss this subject. But the Hebrew Scriptures/Old Testament and Hadeeth say the following:

> Hebrew Scriptures/Old Testament: No one whose testes are crushed or whose member has been cut off shall be admitted into the congregation of the Lord (Deuteronomy 23:2).

> Hadeeth: Muhammad* advised women to not socialize with effeminate men (Bukhari 5.613, 7.162, 7.775, Al-Muwatta 37.5).

☛ Ijtihad: Since the Qur'an is silent on this issue, shall we not assume that it does not consider effeminacy or eunuchs to be an issue–that these men should not be judged on the basis of their sexual development but on their morality and degree of righteousness?

CHAPTER 8. MARRIAGE, DIVORCE, CIRCUMCISION, AND INHERITANCE

I. MARRIAGE

Isn't it true that Muslim men can have up to four wives?
Yes, but only in a special situation:

> Qur'an: If you fear that you shall not be able to deal justly with orphans, marry women of your choice, two or three or four. But if you fear that you will not be able to deal justly (with them), then only one or (a captive) that your right hands possess. That will be more suitable to prevent you from doing injustice (Qur'an 4:3). [Individuals "that your right hand possesses" probably refer to prisoners of war].

Ali (1989) explains this verse as follows: "Notice the conditional clause about orphans introducing the rules about marriage. This verse was revealed after the Battle of Uhud (625 A.D.), when the Muslim community was left with many orphans, widows, and prisoners of war. Their treatment was to be governed by principles of greatest humanity and equity. While that occasion is past, the principle remains: marry (widows and) orphans if you are sure that you will, in that way, protect their interests and property with perfect justice to them and to your (other) dependents (if any). If not, make other arrangements for the orphans."

☞Ijtihad: Would it be far-fetched to suggest that, by linking orphans and women, the Qur'an permits polygamy only to provide shelter and emotional support to unfortunate women–but still advised men to wait for orphan girls to blossom into adulthood before marrying them? Doesn't the fact that Muhammad* betrothed Aisha when she was six or seven but consummated the marriage when she was twelve or thirteen seem to validate this point?

☞Ijtihad: And isn't this point further validated by the following Qur'anic verse, immediately preceding the above-quoted verse:

> Qur'an: To orphans restore their property (when they reach their age), nor substitute (your) worthless things for (their) good ones. And devour not their substance (by mixing it up) (Qur'an 4:2).

☞Ijtihad: Since verse 4:2 deals with orphans and verse 4:3 with orphans and marriage, can we not assume that verse 4:3 is actually referring to the marriage of orphans?

But, isn't it true that many Muslim men practice polygamy in spite of the above-mentioned condition attached to it?
Probably yes. And while statistics on the extent of polygamy among Muslims are not available, probably less than 30% Muslim men might have 2-4 wives nowadays. Do they treat all wives equally? Probably not. Many Muslim countries now have laws governing polygamy.

How many wives did Muhammad* have?
Muhammad* had thirteen (Khadija, Aisha, Sauda, Zainab daughter of Jahsh, Umm Salama, Hafsa, Umm Habiba, Juwayriya, Safiya, Maymuna, Zainab daughter of Khuzayma, Asma, and Amra) (Ishaq, pages 792-794). He* probably contracted these marriages before Qur'anic verse 4:3 was revealed. His first wife, Khadijah, was 17 to 20 years older than he and had had two previous marriages. Of all his wives, only Aisha was previously unmarried; all the others were either divorcees or widows needing protection and support. Muhammad* did not marry after he received the following revelation:

> Qur'an: (O Muhammad) It is not lawful for you (to marry more) women after this (Qur'an 33:52).

Wasn't Aisha a minor when she got married to Muhammad*?
Yes. Aisha was six or seven years old when she was betrothed to
Muhammad*, but the marriage was not consummated until she was
twelve or thirteen. She married him willingly. And apparently it was a
happy marriage. Muhammad* died when she was between 18 and 21
years old (Ishaq, page 792; Bukhari 5.234, 7.64). Child marriage was
not uncommon in the Middle East 1,400 years ago. Even in Hawaii, the
age of "sexual consent" was recently raised from thirteen to fourteen.
While one hears horror stories of young Muslim girls being tricked into
marrying rich old men, such forced marriages are against Islam (Qur'an
4:19). The Qur'an sets no age limit on marriage.

☛Ijtihad: Out of Muhammad's* thirteen wives, twelve were widows
or divorcees–with one being even 18-20 years older. So, shouldn't
devout Muslim men who insist on following literally all of the prophet's
Sunnah, have only one "previously unmarried" maiden among their
wives–with all others being divorcees or widows? And shouldn't their
first wife be even older than the husband?

How many wives did Biblical prophets have?

> Hebrew Scriptures/Old Testament: King Solomon
> loved many foreign women along with the daughter of
> Pharaoh: Moabite, Ammonite, Edomite, Sidonian, and
> Hittite women, from the nations concerning which the
> Lord had said to the Israelites, 'You shall not enter into
> marriage with them, neither shall be they with you; for
> they will surely incline your heart to follow their gods';
> Solomon clung to these in love. Among his wives were
> 700 princesses and 300 concubines, and his wives
> turned away his heart" (1 King 11:1-3) Rehoboam . . .
> took eighteen wives and three score concubines . . . (2
> Chronicles 11:21). David took more wives at Jerusalem
> (1 Chronicles 14:3).
> (Rabbi Magid's note: Solomon [in the Judeo-Christian
> tradition] is not considered a prophet. I am not a Bible

expert but I don't remember any prophets with more than one wife. Actually, very little is mentioned about the wives of the prophets at all.)

(Regina Pfeiffer's note: David and Solomon were living before the final formation of the written texts. Later prophets and writings seem to indicate that having multiple wives and concubines was not the norm–for example, Ezekiel 24:15; the book of Hosea; Malachi 2:14)

New Testament: Jesus* did not have any wife.

How many wives does the Bible permit?

Hebrew Scriptures/Old Testament: This book does not appear to set any limit.

(Rabbi Magid's note: There are no discussions in the Hebrew Scriptures/Old Testament about the number of wives permitted a man. But the practice of more than one wife– prevalent throughout the Middle East– was forbidden in Judaism several hundred years before the birth of Muhammad.)

New Testament: It is better not to marry. But because there is so much immorality, every man should have a wife and every woman, a husband (1 Corinthian 7:1-2).

Does the Qur'an permit forced marriage to slave girls?
No. Even 1,400 years ago, when slavery was common and slaves, especially females, were treated cruelly, the Qur'an forbade men from taking women forcibly. Men were encouraged to free their slaves; also to marry them. And yes! Muslim women could marry male slaves:

Qur'an: You are forbidden to inherit women against their will. Nor should you treat them with harshness that you may take away a part of the dower you have given them–except where they have been guilty of open lewdness. On the contrary, live with them on a footing of kindness and equity. If you take a dislike to them, it may be that you dislike a thing and God brings about through it a great deal of good (Qur'an 4:19). Marry those among you who are single or the virtuous ones among your slaves, male or female. If they are in poverty, God will give them means out of His grace (Qur'an 24:32). A female slave who believes is better (for marriage) than an unbelieving woman, even though she allures you. A male slave who believes is better (for marriage) than an unbeliever, even though he allures you (Qur'an 2:221). Do not force your maids into prostitution when they desire chastity (Qur'an 24:33).

Does the Bible permit forced marriage?

Hebrew Scriptures/Old Testament: When you go to war against your enemies, and the Lord your God has delivered them to your hands and you have taken them captive, and you see among the captives a beautiful woman and you desire to make her your wife, then you shall bring her to your home, and she shall shave her head and pare her nails; and she shall put the raiment of her captivity from off her, and shall remain in your house and bewail her father and mother a full month: and after that you shall go in unto her, and be her husband and she, your wife (Deuteronomy 22:10-13). (The elders) commanded the children of Benjamin saying: Go and lie in wait in the vineyards. And see, and behold, if the daughters of Shiloh come out to dance in dances, then you come out of the vineyards, and catch you every man his wife of the daughters of Shiloh, and go to the land of Benjamin (Judges 21: 20-21).

(Rabbi Magid's note: Taking female captives was a common practice 3,000+ years ago; but notice that even they were treated respectfully, given time to mourn, and then married. The practice of taking female slaves ended shortly after the time of Solomon, 2,900 years ago.)

New Testament: This subject is not discussed.

Isn't mut'a (temporary marriage) permitted in Islam?
In Islam, marriage is not "made in heaven". It is a civil contract in which the terms of divorce, should one occur, are spelled out in the marriage contract. The difference between mut'a and divorce would be the intention: whether it is to be a "permanent" arrangement (which could end in divorce later) or, from inception, it is to be a temporary arrangement by mutual agreement. God alone knows what is in people's hearts. Mut'a is not discussed in the Qur'an, and there are mixed signals in Hadeeth. As we saw in Chapter 3, mut'a was permitted up to a certain point (Battle of Khaibar, A.D. 628, or up to 18 years after Muhammad* started receiving revelations) (Bukhari 5.527, 7.432, 7.50, 9.91, Chapter 1). However, since some Shias consider mut'a to be lawful, it is still practiced in several Shia communities around the world (Ruquia Jafri, personal communication).

Hadeeth: Once, two men vied for the hand of the same woman (for contracting temporary marriage). She asked: "What dower would you give me?" Both of them offered their cloaks. She took the younger man, saying: "Well, you and your cloak are sufficient for me." This man remained with her for three nights (Muslim 3252).

☞ Ijtihad: Since the woman bargained and received some goods in return for the temporary marriage, could this event be classified as a form of prostitution? Did these incidents take place after mut'a had already been disallowed (Chapter 1)? God knows best.

Proponents of mut'a explain that it provides a healthy biological outlet for individuals when away from home. They explain that it is not prostitution because the man is still responsible for any children born out of this arrangement.

> Hadeeth: A companion of the prophet reported: "We used to participate in the holy wars carried on by the Prophet. [Since we would be gone for long], the prophet allowed us to marry a woman (temporarily) by giving her even a garment, and then he recited: "O you who believe! Do not make unlawful the good things which Allah has made lawful for you" (Bukhari 6.139).

What does the Qur'an say about polyandry (one woman having several husbands simultaneously)?
Polyandry is not discussed in the Qur'an. However, consider the following Hadeeth:

> Hadeeth: Three men had sexual relation with the same woman "during a single state of purity." [The meaning is unclear: does this refer to the woman's one monthly cycle?] Later, all three came to Ali claiming to be the father of the child born to that woman. Perplexed, the only thing Ali could do was to award the child to one of them by drawing lots. When Ali reported this to Muhammad*, the latter laughed so much that his canine or molar teeth appeared (Abu Dawood 2262, 2263).

☞Ijtihad: Was this polyandry? Or were these three temporary marriages (mut'a) within this short period? Or was this adultery? If so, why were these men and the woman not punished for adultery (See Chapter 9)? All of them openly acknowledged their sexual relations with her Or is this Hadeeth false?

II. DIVORCE

Isn't it true that Muslims can divorce their wives simply by saying "I divorce you" three times?
It does take three pronouncements, but these are to be separated by menstrual cycles (iddah). This provides an opportunity for well-wishers to seek reconciliation. It also allows time to ascertain if the wife is pregnant (in which case the divorce would be delayed):

> Qur'an: A (pronouncement of) divorce is only permissible twice: after that, the parties should either hold together on equitable terms or separate with kindness (Qur'an 2:229). If you fear a breach between them, appoint (two) arbiters one from his family and the other from hers. If they wish for peace, God will cause their reconciliation (Qur'an 4:35).

How is the wife to be treated during this iddah period?

> Qur'an: Let the women live (in iddah) in the same style as you live according to your means: annoy them not so as to restrict them (Qur'an 65:6-7). Do not turn away (from your wife) altogether so as to leave her hanging (in the air). If you come to a friendly understanding, God is oft-forgiving, most merciful. But if they disagree (and must part), God will provide abundance for all from His all-reaching Bounty (4:129-30).

And what happens when the iddah is over?

> Qur'an: When you divorce women and they fulfil the term (of 'iddah), either take them back on equitable terms or set them free on equitable terms; but do not take them back to injure them or to take undue advantage. If anyone does that, he wrongs his own soul (Qur'an 2:231).

How are the terms of divorce decided?
The Qur'an suggests that, at the time of the wedding, the couple decide what the wife would receive should divorce occur. Men are not to take back any gifts from their former wives. Also, divorce carries no stigma.

> Qur'an: It is not lawful for you (men) to take back any of your gifts (from your wives) except when both parties fear that they would be unable to keep the limits ordained by God (Qur'an 2:229).

Does the wife receive any maintenance allowance after the divorce?

> Qur'an: For divorced women, maintenance (should be provided) on a reasonable (scale). This is a duty on the righteous (Qur'an 2:241).

Can the wife file for/initiate divorce?

> Qur'an: Women shall have rights similar to the rights against them according to what is equitable (Qur'an 2:228). If a wife fears cruelty or desertion on her husband's part, there is no blame if they arrange an amicable settlement between themselves; and such settlement is best; even though men's souls are swayed by greed (Qur'an 4:128).

How does the Bible deal with divorce?

> Hebrew Scriptures/Old Testament: When a man has taken a wife and married her, and it comes to pass that she finds no favor in his eyes because he has found some uncleanliness in her, then he writes her a bill of divorcement, and gives it in her hand, and send her out of his house (Deuteronomy 24:1).
> (Rabbi Magid's note: This practice ended 2,500 years ago–1,500 years before Islam).

New Testament: It has been said, whosoever shall put away his wife, let him give her a writing of divorcement. But I say unto you, that whosoever shall put away his wife, saving for the cause of fornication, causes her to commit adultery. And whosoever shall marry her that is divorced, commits adultery (Matthew: 31-32; Luke 16:18). And unto the married man I command, yet not I, but the Lord, Let not the wife depart from her husband. But if she departs, let her remain unmarried or be reconciled to her husband: and let not the husband put away his wife. But to the rest speak I, not the Lord: If any brother has a wife that believes not, and she be pleased to dwell with him, let him not put her away. And the woman which has a husband who believes not, And if he be pleased to dwell with her, let her not leave him. For the unbelieving husband is sanctified by the wife; and the unbelieving wife is sanctified by the husband: else were your children unclean; but now are they holy (1 Corinthians 7:10-14).

According to the Bible, can the wife file for divorce? Also, does the ex-wife get any maintenance allowance after divorce?
These matters are also not discussed in the Bible.
(Rabbi Magid's note: The post-Biblical literature/practice reverses this with the introduction of the Ketubah, or Jewish marriage document, a legal text outlining the rights of women, financial issues, etc. It is the first such document in world history. It was created 500 years before Islam and still exists today.

The New Testament permits divorce only if the wife commits adultery. What if the man commits adultery?
This matter is not discussed in the New Testament.

III. CIRCUMCISION AND FEMALE GENITAL MUTILATION

Doesn't the Qur'an prescribe male and female circumcision?
No. Even the practice of male circumcision is not mentioned in the Qur'an. We find this nly in some Hadeeth. For example:

> Hadeeth: Muhammad* included circumcision among five *fitra* ("good practices") (Bukhari 7.777, 8.312, 8.313, Al-Muwatta 49.3, Abu Dawood 5251). He also advised a woman who performed circumcision to not cut severely "as that is better for the woman and more desirable for her husband" (Abu Dawood 5251).

It is assumed that she performed this on females. We also learn that Abraham* performed circumcision on himself at age 80 (Bukhari 8.313; Fiqh-us-Sunnah 1.21a). Male circumcision is recommended by some Muslim schools and not by others (Fiqh-us-Sunnah 1.21a). Female circumcision is mentioned neither in the Qur'an nor Hadeeth. And while male circumcision is practiced traditionally by all Muslims, female circumcision is found only in some societies; it predates Islam.

Was Muhammad circumcised?*
Probably. Circumcision was a common Arab practice (Bukhari 1.6). Some Muslims believe that Muhammad* was born circumcised.

What does the Bible say regarding circumcision?
Hebrew Scriptures/Old Testament require it; the New Testament opposes it.

> Hebrew Scriptures/Old Testament: Circumcision is required of all Hebrew males on the 8th day after birth (for example, Genesis 17:10); and Joshua circumcised all the sons of Israel (Joshua 5:3).

> New Testament: "If you get circumcised, Christ shall profit you nothing" (Galatians 5:2). Circumcision of the

heart (that is, leading a righteous life) is more important (Romans 2:25-29).

IV. INHERITANCE

(A) Wills

How does Islam deal with inheritance? Do females get any share?
Yes. Females can even get all, if it is so willed. The Qur'an suggests strongly that people write their wills ahead of time to ensure that the property goes to the "right" individuals in accordance with their wishes. Whom to give and how much is left open:

> Qur'an: It is prescribed when death approaches anyone, if he leaves any goods, that he makes a bequest to parents and next of kin according to reasonable usage; this is due from the God-fearing (Qur'an 2:180; 5:106).

> Hadeeth: Someone asked Muhammad*, "I have property and only my daughter inherits from me. Shall I give two thirds of my property in charity?" Muhammad* responded, "No." "Half?" "No. A third, and a third is a lot. Leaving heirs rich is better than leaving them poor" (Al Muwatta 37.4).

> Hadeeth: The Messenger said, "It is the duty of a Muslim man who has something to be given as a bequest not to spend two nights without writing a will about it." (Al Muwatta 37.1).

(b) LAW OF INHERITANCE

What happens if a person dies without writing a will?

> Qur'an: God (thus) directs you as regards your children's (inheritance): to the male a portion equal to that of two females . . . (see Qur'an 4:11 for details).

Those who die should bequeath for their widows a
year's maintenance and residence (Qur'an 2:240).

When there is no will, females receive half of what males get. Why?
This level of inheritance going to females was a big improvement over
Biblical injunction and the prevailing cultural practice in the Middle
East at that time. There is also another reason: Since the husband is
responsible for maintaining the family, his wife shares in his wealth; but
she does not have to share with her husband the wealth she inherits
from her family. This contrasts with the practice which prevailed in
Europe and America till only a few centuries ago that when a woman
married, all her property was transferred to the husband.

☛Ijtihad: Shouldn't the Muslim law of inheritance be brought into
conformity with the following Qur'anic commandments discussed
above? (1) Individuals <u>must</u> prepare their wills and specify who gets
how much; they could even leave everything to their daughters and/or
other females if they so desired (Qur'an 2:180 and 5:106; also Al-
Muwatta 37.4); (2) If people die without having prepared a will, then
Qur'anic verses 4:11 and 2:240 would apply.

How does the Bible deal with bequests and inheritance?
According to the Hebrew Scriptures/Old Testament, only sons share
in the inheritance, with the firstborn getting double the share of the
others. Generally, daughters do not get any share (except when there
is no son–but only if they marry within their own tribe. See below) .

> Hebrew Scriptures/Old Testament: If a man has two
> wives, one loved and the other unloved, and both the
> loved and unloved have borne him sons, but the
> firstborn is the son of the unloved one–when he wills
> his property to his sons, he may not treat as firstborn
> the son of the loved one in disregard of the son of the
> unloved who is the older. Instead, he must accept the
> firstborn, the son of the unloved one, and allot to him
> a double portion of all he possesses; since he is the first

fruit of his vigor, the birthright is his due (Deuteronomy 21:15-17).

New Testament: Does not appear to deal with this subject.
(Regina Pfeiffer's note: Inheritance would have followed the Judaic law in early Christianity, then Roman law as Christianity became part of Roman society. The Christian scriptures were not concerned about inheritance partly because of this reason and also because in the early Christian movement (about 40-70 C.E.), the community felt that Jesus, the Messiah, would be returning soon, during their lifetime. Thus there would be no urgency to deal with bequests and inheritance).

But what happens if there are no sons?
Only in this case, daughters may inherit their parents' property–but only if they married within their own tribe.

Hebrew Scriptures/Old Testament: (Concerning the daughters of Zelophahed): They may marry anyone they wish provided they marry into a clan of their father's tribe. No inheritance of the Israelites may pass from one tribe to another, but the Israelites must remain bound each to the ancestral portion of his tribe. Every daughter among the Israelite tribes who inherit a share (of property) must marry someone from a clan of her father's tribe, in order that every Israelite may keep his ancestral share. Thus no inheritance shall pass over from one tribe to another, but the Israelite tribes shall remain bound each to its portion (Numbers 36:8-9).
(Rabbi Magid's note: Remember the context: Each tribe of Israel was given a certain parcel of land. The inheritance [law cited here] was designed to keep the tribes's land intact).

CHAPTER 9. ADULTERY, HOMOSEXUALITY, AND LESBIANISM

I. ADULTERY

Isn't it true that punishment for adultery in Islam is death and that usually only the woman gets punished?
No. One finds death for adultery in the Hebrew Scriptures/Old Testament. And while the New Testament's injunction virtually ensures no punishment, the Qur'an takes the "middle ground."

> Hebrew Scriptures/Old Testament: If a man commits adultery with a married woman, committing adultery with another man's wife, the adulterer and adulteress shall be put to death (Leviticus 20:10).
> (Rabbi Magid's note: Remember: adultery has to do with sex between/with married individuals. Having sex with a single woman was considered a way to marry her, as long as it was consensual.)

> New Testament: "He that is without sin, let him cast the first stone" (John 8:7). (Since most of us are not "without sin," it would be difficult to find the person who would cast the first stone.)

> Qur'an: The woman and the man guilty of adultery or fornication: flog each of them with a hundred stripes. . . . Let no man guilty of adultery or fornication marry any but a woman similarly guilty or an unbeliever; nor let any but such a man or an unbeliever marry such a woman. To believers, such a thing is forbidden (Qur'an 24: 2-3.). Women impure are for men impure and men impure are for women impure; and women of purity are

for men of purity and men of purity are for women of purity (Qur'an 24:26).

☛Ijtihad: Don't Qur'anic verses 24:2-3 clarify that the guilty are to survive this punishment? And doesn't verse 24:26 reconfirm this by stating that impure men can marry impure women?

Hadeeth: The adulterer who has been flogged shall not marry save the one like him (Abu Dawood 2047).

☛Ijtihad: Couldn't the "similarly guilty"/"impure person" be the person's adultery partner? Thus, isn't the Qur'an providing them both with an opportunity to start life afresh after their punishment?

☛ Ijtihad: Also, as we saw on page 49, doesn't the fact that Abu Bakra survived the punishment of 80 stripes [for accusing a chaste woman falsely] show that whipping was more a psychological punishment than a physical one?

☛ Ijtihad: Isn't therefore flogging to be more a symbolic gesture? For example, the prophet ordered a sick person found guilty of adultery to be whipped only once, with a stalk of a palm tree having a hundred twigs (Tirmidhi 3574). Also, a book was often placed under the flogger's arm to limit hand-raising and minimize injury (Justice Agha Ali Hyder, quoting Maulana Maudoodi, <u>in</u> FSC, 1981).

Then why have some Muslims been killed for adultery?
This is based on some Hadeeth–and runs contrary to other Hadeeth and the Qur'an. Also, the punishment prescribed varied. These are summarized below, with details and references indicated on the next two pages (which may be skipped by those not interested in details)

A. Punishment for adultery (illicit sex committed by married people): Muhammad* prescribed *rajam* (death by stoning) in five cases, 100 lashes plus *rajam* on another occasion (Case 6), and prescribed no punishment in another three cases (Cases 7-9).

B. Punishment for fornication (illicit sex involving unmarried people): Muhammad* prescribed 100 lashes in one case (Case 10) (50 lashes to a slave girl, Case 11), and 100 lashes plus one-year exile in another (Case 12). No punishment was prescribed in another case (Case 13).

Details of punishments awarded by Muhammad* for adultery and fornication

I. Adultery cases (involving married persons)

(A) Punishment: rajam
Case 1 involved a Jewish couple whose case was brought before Muhammad* by the leaders of the Jewish tribe. Muhammad* based his judgment on the Hebrew Scriptures/Old Testament (Abu Dawood 4435; Al-Muwatta 41.1; Bukhari 2.413, 6.79, 8.809, 8.825; Muslim 4214);
Case 2 involved a confessed adulterer (Al-Muwatta 41.4; Bukhari 8.805-806, 8.810, 8.813, 8.814; and Muslim 4198). (Was the woman also punished?)
Case 3 involved a confessed adulteress. (Her unmarried paramour was given 100 lashes and one-year exile) (Al-Muwatta 41.6; Bukhari 8.815, 8.821, 8.826, 8.842; Abu Dawood 4429);
Case 4 involved a pregnant woman who confessed adultery, after she delivered her baby (Al-Muwatta 41.5; Abu Dawood 4426; Muslim 4205, 4207);
Case 5. Muhammad* declared that the illegitimate child belongs to the husband, and the stone "belongs" to the adulterer (Bukhari 8.807, 8.808).

(B) Punishment: 100 lashes plus rajam
Case 6. Muhammad* reportedly declared that the punishment for adultery was 100 lashes plus rajam (Muslim 4191).

(C) <u>Punishment: None</u>

Case 7. Three men had sexual intercourse with the same woman "in a single state of purity." Later, each claimed to be the father of the child born to the woman. When Muhammad* learned of this, he laughed so much that his canine or molar teeth showed (Abu Dawood 2262, 2263). None of them was punished.

Case 8. A man found his wife with another man. He had no other witness and the wife denied the adultery. No punishment was prescribed. But Muhammad* permitted the couple to get divorced (Bukhari 7.230).

Case 9. Muhammad* prescribed rajam to Ma'iz, a confessed adulterer. When stones started injuring him, he fled–but was caught and killed. When Muhammad* heard this, he asked, "Why did you not leave him alone? Perhaps he might have repented and been forgiven by God." (Abu Dawood 4405; Tirmidhi 3565).

II. Fornication: (involving unmarried persons)

(A) <u>Punishment: 100 lashes; (50 lashes to a slave girl)</u>.

Case 10. A fornicator was whipped; but the woman he named denied it and so escaped punishment (Abu Dawood 4423, 4451).

Case 11. Fifty lashes were given to a slave girl and warned that repeat offenders would be sold "even for a hair rope" (Bukhari 8.822, 8.823).

(B) <u>Punishment: 100 lashes plus one-year exile</u>

Case 12. Awarded to an unmarried person (Bukhari 8.818, 8.819; Al-Muwatta 41.13). (See also Case No. 3).

(C) <u>Punishment: None</u>

Case 13. Muhammad* applauded Ali (later the fourth Caliph) who did not whip an adulterous slave woman because he feared he might kill her (as she had recently given birth) (Muslim 4224).

Case 14 A slave-girl complained that her master forced her into prostitution. Subsequently, the Qur'an prohibited this practice (verse 24:33) (Abu-Dawood 2304).

☛ Ijtihad: Why do we have these major differences in punishment for similar offences?

☛ Ijtihad: Since differences exist, shouldn't we do Ijtihad before killing anyone for adultery? Couldn't the shortcomings suggested in Chapter 3 help explain these differences?

☛ Ijtihad: Since many Hadeeth lack dates, can't we assume that Muhammad* followed the Torah, until such time that he was revealed Qur'anic verse 24:2-3 quoted above? As we saw earlier, Mouhammad* specifically used the Torah to prescribe *rajam* in Case 1.

> Hadeeth: (Case 15). One person asked another person, "Did God's Apostle carry out *rajam*?" The second replied, "Yes." The first asked, "Before the revelation of Surah Al-Nur or after it?" The second replied, "I don't know." (Bukhari 8.804). [Surah Nur is Surah 24, cited above].

Case involving the prophet's wife (Case 16):
Ishaq (page 496), writing about a 100 years before Bukhari compiled his Hadeeth, described the incident surrounding the rumor that Aisha had possibly committed adultery. The prophet told Aisha: "Aisha, you know what people say about you. Fear God and if you have done wrong as men say, then repent toward God, for He accepts repentance from His slaves." This took place in 6 A.H. The fact that Muhammad* did not mention that Aisha could be stoned to death (in case she was guilty) suggests that he had perhaps already stopped prescribing this punishment. Indeed, while the punishment of 100 lashes for adultery

occurs in Qur'anic verses 24:2-3, Aisha's case is mentioned only a few verses later (Qur'an 24:11-20). However, here are Umar's views regarding punishment for adultery:

> Hadeeth: Umar (the second caliph) declared: ". . . Among what God revealed to Muhammad* was the verse of rajam, and we did recite this verse, understood it, and memorized it. God's Apostle carried out the punishment of stoning and so did we after him. I am afraid that after some time, somebody will say, 'By God, we do not find the verse of the rajam in God's Book,' and thus they will go astray by leaving an obligation which God has revealed. The punishment of rajam is to be inflicted to any married person (male and female), who commits illegal sexual intercourse, if the required evidence is available or there is conception or confession" (Bukhari 8.817).

☞Ijtihad: Based on Umar's assertion, are these not the only conclusions we can draw? (a) a verse prescribing *rajam* may have existed in the Qur'an earlier; (b) since we do not find it there now, it must have been later abrogated by God; and (c) the verses that may have replaced this verse were probably verses 24:2-3 (or whole Surah Al-Nur). Since the prophet always changed his actions to conform to incoming revelations, isn't it possible therefore that he stopped prescribing *rajam* after Surah No. 24 was revealed? All Hadeeth prescribing *rajam* must, therefore, pedate the revelation of Surah 24.

Ishaq (page 684-5, footnote) offers the following discussion: "If it [Omar's statement that a verse prescribing rajam for adultery] was part of the Qur'an, it is difficult to see where it stood originally. Muslim authorities suggest Surah 33, but the rhyme forbids this; and Surah 24, but there the punishment is scourging [whipping]. Most commentators hold that the verse is one of those that were afterwards abrogated, while others say it was accidentally lost due to a domestic animal eating the part of the page on which the revelation was written. . . . However, if the traditional form of Umar's speech . . . is authentic, it remains to be explained why Umar, who was a most truthful man, should have publicly stated in the strongest possible terms that the verse was to be read in the Qur'an."

☞Ijtihad: If, as God has promised, the Qur'an will remain intact forever, isn't it blasphemous to suggest that a domestic animal may have accidentally eaten the paper on which any verse was written? Or to suggest that we should practice *rajam* because it was in the Qur'an at one time–even though we do not see it in the Qur'an now?

Can women be punished on hearsay evidence?
No. The Qur'an accepts only the following evidence: (a) Four witnesses; (b) Confession; or (c) Pregnancy, but not from rape.

A) Acceptable evidence: Four witnesses (Qur'an 24:4).
> Hadeeth: Case 17. Muhammad* could not punish another woman as he lacked four witnesses (Bukhari 7.230, 8.838, 8.839).
> Case 18. Also, charges cannot be based on circumstantial evidence. Thus, when someone told Muhammad* that he saw his wife with another person, the prophet asked him to produce four witnesses (Al-Muwatta 41.7). Since he could not produce four witnesses, the wife was not punished.

Is it possible to get four witnesses to an illegal sex act?
Probably not–especially when we are not permitted to force entry into any person's house or hotel room, or even to peep at what people might be doing behind closed doors:

> Qur'an: Do not enter houses other than your own until you have asked permission and saluted those in them. . . . If you find no one in the house, do not enter until permission is given to you. If you are asked to go back, go back. That makes for greater purity for you. It is no

fault on your part to enter houses not used for living, which serves some (other) use for you (24:27-29).

Hadeeth: Muhammad* said, "If anyone removes a curtain and looks inside a house before receiving permission and sees anything which should not be seen, he has committed an unlawful offence. . . . But if a man passes a door which has no curtain and is not shut and looks in, he has committed no sin, for the sin pertains only to the people inside" (Tirmidhi 3526).

The following underscores Muhammad's* sensitivity to privacy:

Hadeeth: When anyone is away from his house for a long time, he should not return to his family at night (Bukhari 7.171). He who sees something which should be kept hidden and conceals it, it will be like one who has brought to life a girl buried alive (Abu Dawood 4873).

Case 19: Muhammad* warned people to "cover up" their illegal sexual activities; else they would receive the prescribed punishment (Al-Muwatta 41.12)

Thus, not only are we forbidden from entering someone's house, even a hotel room, forcibly (for example, to see if a couple committing adultery), but if, by chance, we see them committing adultery, we are to not broadcast that fact. Let it be to God to decide their punishment.

B) Acceptable Evidence: Confession (see Cases 1, 2, 3, and 7, 8, 9).
    Case 20: A person admitted his adultery to Abu Bakar
    and Umar. Both advised him not to tell Muhammad*.
    However, he also told Muhammad*. He was then
    stoned (Al Muwatta 41.2).

C) Acceptable Evidence: Pregnancy, but not from rape
  Case 21. There needs to be clear proof of pregnancy
  (Al-Muwatta 41.8)–but not from rape.

☛ Ijtihad: Should a pregnant woman, who claims to have been raped, be punished? Shouldn't her oath, invoking the wrath of God if she is lying, be accepted? After all, such an oath is accepted from a wife when her husband accuses her of infidelity (see below). How many maidservants would have the courage to accuse their masters of raping them. Shouldn't the woman be given the benefit of doubt–as is compassionately advised by the prophet in the following Hadeeth?

> Hadeeth: Muhammad* advised: Avoid inflicting the prescribed penalty on Muslims as much as you can, and if there is any way out, let a man go. It is better for a leader to make a mistake in forgiving than to make a mistake in punishing (Tirmidhi 3570).

But isn't it easy to punish a woman just on hearsay?
Not according to the Qur'an. This Book takes a serious view of individuals who accuse women but have no witnesses:

> Qur'an: Those who launch a charge against chaste women, and do not produce four witnesses (to support their allegation): Flog them each with 80 stripes and reject their evidence ever after (Qur'an 24:4).

What if a man accuses his wife of adultery but has no witnesses?
Her oath of innocence is superior to his oath of accusation:

> Qur'an: And for those who launch a charge against their spouses and have (in support) no evidence but their own, their solitary evidence (can be received) if they bear witness four times (with an oath) by God that they are solemnly telling the truth; And the fifth (oath) (should be) that they solemnly invoke the curse of God

on themselves if they tell a lie. But it would avoid the
punishment on the wife if she bears witness four times
(with an oath) by God that (her husband) is telling a lie;
And the fifth (oath) should be that she solemnly invokes
the wrath of God on herself if (her accuser) is telling
the truth (Qur'an 24:6-10.).

*According to the Bible, how can a wife prove her innocence when
accused of adultery by her husband?*

Hebrew Scriptures/Old Testament: And the Lord spoke
unto Moses, saying: Speak to the Israelite people and
say to them:
If any man's wife has gone astray and broken faith with
him in that a man has had carnal relations with her
unbeknown to her husband, and she keeps secret the
fact that she has defiled herself without being forced,
and there is no witness against her–but a fit of jealousy
comes over him and he is wrought up about the wife
who has defiled herself; or if a fit of jealousy comes
over one and he is wrought up about his wife although
she has not defiled herself–the man shall bring his wife
to the priest. And he shall bring as an offering for her
one-tenth of an ephah of barley flour. No oil shall be
poured upon it and no frankincense shall be laid on it,
for it is a meal offering of jealousy, a meal offering of
remembrance which recalls wrongdoing.
The priest shall bring her forward and have her stand
before the Lord. The priest shall take sacral water in an
earthen vessel and, taking some of the earth that is on
the floor in the Tabernacle, the priest shall put it in the
water. After he has made the woman stand before the
Lord, the priest shall bare the woman's head and place
upon her hands the meal offering of remembrance,
which is a meal offering of jealousy. And in the priest's
hands shall be the water of bitterness that induces the

spell. The priest shall adjure the woman saying to her, "If no man has lain with you, or if you have not gone astray in defilement while married to your husband, be immune from harm from this water of bitterness that induces the spell. But if you have gone astray while married to your husband and have defiled yourself, if a man other than your husband has had carnal relations with you"–here the priest shall administer the curse of adjuration to the woman, as the priest goes on to say to the woman–"may the Lord make you a curse and an imprecation among your people, as the Lord causes your thigh to sag and your belly to distend; may this water that induces the spell enter your body, causing the belly to distend and the thigh to sag." And the woman shall say, "Amen, amen."

The priest shall put these curses down in writing and rub it off into the water of bitterness. He has to make the woman drink the water of bitterness that induces the spell, so that the spell-inducing water may enter into her to bring on the bitterness. Then the priest shall take from the woman's hand the meal offering of jealousy, elevate the meal offering before the Lord, and present it on the altar. The priest shall scoop out of the meal offering a token part of it and turn it into smoke on the altar. Last, he shall make the woman drink the water.

Once he has made her drink the water–if she has defiled herself by breaking faith with her husband, the spell-inducing water shall enter into her to bring on bitterness, so that her belly shall distend and her thigh shall sag; and the woman shall become a curse among her people. But if the woman has not defiled herself and is pure, she shall be unharmed and able to retain seed. This is the ritual in cases of jealousy, when a woman goes astray while married to her husband and defiles herself, or when a fit of jealousy comes over a man, and

he is wrought up over his wife: the woman shall be made to stand before the Lord and the priest shall carry out all this ritual with her. The man shall be clear of guilt, but that woman shall suffer for the guilt (Numbers 5:11-31)
(Rabbi Magid's note: This practice ended 1,000 years before Islam began).

New Testament: This subject is not discussed.
(Regina Pfeiffer's note: Christian scripture does not address this partly because it would adhere to the Mosaic law).

Do Hadeeth on adultery impact the lives of Muslims nowadays?
Yes indeed. Consider the following diametrically opposite judicial rulings: In 1981, Pakistan's Shariat Court, using the Qur'an as authority, declared rajam to be repugnant to Islam and asserted that the punishment for adultery (whether by married or unmarried persons) was to be 100 lashes (FSC, 1981). But this was reversed a year later when the Shariat Review Court declared that fornicators are to receive 100 lashes each, and adulterers are to be stoned to death (FSC, 1982).

☛ Ijtihad: Which ruling should Muslims follow? In matters of life and death, shouldn't Muslims follow the Hadeeth (Tirmidhi 3570) quoted on page 157?

Is there any room for prayers and forgiveness?
Hadeeth: A man confessed to Muhammad* that he had committed "a legally punishable sin" and asked to be punished. The prophet did not ask him what he had done. After prayers, the man again reminded Muhammad* of his confession. The prophet asked, "Haven't you prayed with us?' He said, "Yes." The prophet said, "God has forgiven your sin" (Bukhari 8.812).

☛ Ijtihad: Isn't it possible that Hadeeth suggesting prayers and seeking God's forgiveness pertain to the time <u>after</u> Muhammad* received Qur'anic verses 24:2-3?

How does illicit sex "measure up" against other vices?

> Hadeeth: Muhammad* said that "a dirham which a man knowingly receives in usury is more serious than thirty-six acts of illegal sexual intercourse" (Tirmidhi 2825); that "whoever dies without worshiping anything but God, will enter Paradise– even if he committed theft or illegal sexual intercourse" (Bukhari 2.329, 8.450); and that "an adulterer is not considered to be a believer when he commits illegal sexual intercourse, and [but] the gate of repentance remains open" (Bukhari 8.800B, 8.801).

Did prostitution exist in the prophet's time in Arabia?

> Hadeeth: Case 22. Muhammad* declared the earnings of prostitutes to be illegal (Abu Dawood 3414, 3421,3477; Al Muwatta 31.68, 54.42; Bukhari 3.439, 3.440, 3.482, 3.483, 7.258, 7.259, 7.260, 7.656, 7.845; Muslim 3806).
>
> Case 23. When a dog was about to die of thirst, an Israelite prostitute filled her shoe with water and gave it to the dog. So God forgave her. (Bukhari 4.538, 4.673; Fiqh-us-Sunnah 3.104).
>
> Case 24. A man named Marthad had illicit relations with a prostitute named Inaq. When Marthad asked the prophet if he could marry her, Muhammad* responded negatively (Abu Dawood 2046). (Note: Apparently neither Marthad nor Inaq was flogged).
>
> Case 25: Muhammad* said, "A man unknowingly gave his charity first to a thief, then to an adulteress, and then to a rich man. He was unhappy. Then someone

said: The alms you gave to the thief might make him abstain from stealing; that given to the adulteress might make her abstain from adultery, and that to the wealthy man might make him take a lesson from it and spend his wealth which God has given him (Bukhari 2.502).

II. HOMOSEXUALITY AND LESBIANISM

According to the Qur'an, are homosexuals and lesbians to be killed? That is in the Hebrew Scriptures/Old Testament; the Qur'an suggests house arrest; and the New Testament does not address this issue:

> Hebrew Scriptures/Old Testament: If a man lies with a man as one lies with a woman, the two of them have done an abhorrent thing; they shall be put to death–their bloodguilt is upon them (Leviticus 20: 13).

> New Testament: This matter is not discussed.

> Qur'an: [The prophet] Lut* said to his people: "Do you commit lewdness such as no people in creation (ever) committed before you? For you practice your lusts on men in preference to women: you are indeed a people transgressing beyond bounds" (Qur'an 7:80-81).

> Qur'an: If any of your women are guilty of lewdness, take the evidence of four (reliable) witnesses. If they testify, confine them to houses until death claims them or God ordains some (other) way. If two men are guilty of lewdness, punish them both. If they repent and amend leave them alone (Qur'an: 4:15-16).

☞ Ijtihad: (1) Isn't the assumption in verses 4:15-16 that lewd men are to be punished the same as lewd women? (2) Then, should the last sentence apply to both men and women–especially since God had indicated earlier that He may show some other way?

Chapter 10. Food, Drink, Gambling, and Usury   163

CHAPTER 10. FOOD, DRINK, GAMBLING, AND USURY

I. FOOD

Do Muslims have any dietary restrictions?

Qur'an: Forbidden to you (for food) are: carrion, blood, the flesh of swine; that on which has been invoked the name of other than God; that which has been killed by strangling, violent blow, headlong fall, or by being gored to death; that which has been (partly) eaten by some wild animal–unless you are able to slaughter it (in due form)–and that which is sacrificed on stone (altars). (Forbidden) also is the division (of meat) by raffling with arrows (Qur'an 5:3, 16:115). Eat not of (meats) on which God's name has not been pronounced (Qur'an 6:121).

And what is "lawful food" for Muslims to eat?

Qur'an: Eat of the good things that We have provided for you and be grateful to God, if it is Him you worship. He has only forbidden you carrion, and blood, and the flesh of swine, and that on which any other name has been invoked besides that of God (Qur'an 2:172-173, 6:145). Lawful unto you (for food) are all four-footed animals with the exceptions named: but animals of the chase are forbidden while you are in the Sacred Precincts or in pilgrim garb. (Qur'an 5:1, 5:4, 5:88, 16:114). This day are (all) things good and pure made lawful unto you. The food of the People of the Book is lawful unto you and yours is lawful unto them

(Qur'an 5:5). Do not make unlawful the good things which God has made lawful for you (Qur'an 5:87, 6:118-119).

But what happens if the only food available is "unlawful" food?

Qur'an: But, if one is forced by necessity, without wilful disobedience nor transgressing due limits, then is he guiltless (Qur'an 2:173).

What is "halal meat" and what is its importance?
"Halal" means lawful. We have two relevant verses regarding food: (1) Verse 2:173 clarifies that prohibited meat is one on which the name of any deity other than God was invoked; (2) Verse 6:121 states the only meat permitted is one on which God's name was pronounced while being slaughtered. Many Muslims will not eat any meat which is not "halal"–not slaughtered following some prescribed rituals. The Qur'an does not prescribe any rituals for slaughtering, but some Hadeeth do. This would be similar to Jews eating only "kosher" meat.

What should Muslims do?
☞ Ijtihad: Since slaughtering of animals in non-Muslim countries takes place mechanically and in bulk (with no name being taken while slaughtering), shouldn't Muslims living in non-Muslim countries seek guidance from the following two Hadeeth?

Hadeeth: Muhammad* said, "I have been sent with an easy and straight-forward religion" (Fiqh-us-Sunnah 2:153). ". . . So do not be extremists . . ." (Bukhari 1.38).

Hadeeth: The prophet was asked, "Some desert people bring us meat, but we do not know whether the name of God was mentioned over it or not." The prophet said, "Mention the name of God over it and eat." (Al Muwatta 24.1; Bukhari 3.273, 7.415, 9.495).

Are any dietary restrictions mentioned in the Bible?

> Hebrew Scriptures/Old Testament: (A) What you can eat: All animals with parted hoofs, which are cloven footed, and which chew the cud; marine animals which have fins and scales, every flying creeping thing that goes on all four feet (such as locusts, beetles, grasshopper).
>
> (B) What you cannot eat: (a) Animals which chew the cud, but their hoofs are not divided: camel, coney, hare; (b) Animals with divided hoofs which are cloven footed, but which do not chew the cud: swine; (c) Marine animals which have no fins and scales; (d) Birds: eagle, ossifrage, osprey; vulture and kite; raven, owl, night hawk, cuckow; (e) Owls, cormorant, swan, pelican, gier eagle, stork, heron, lapwing, bat; (f) Fowls that creep; (g) Other flying creeping things having four feet (except those permitted above); (h) Animals which go on paws; (i) Creeping things such as mouse, tortoise, ferret, chameleon, lizard, snail, mole; (j) Animals which die natural death, even among those which are permissible to eat.
>
> (C) Containers: These can become unclean by contact with the prohibited animals (based on Deuteronomy 11:1-47).

> New Testament: For it seemed good to the Holy Ghost, and to us, to lay upon you no greater burden than these necessary things: That you abstain from meats offered to idols, and from blood, and from things strangled, and from fornication: from which if you keep yourselves, you shall do well (Acts 15: 28-29).
>
> (Regina Pfeiffer's note: The historical context should be noted: Initially, Gentiles who wished to become Christian needed to adhere to the Judaic laws, such as dietary restrictions and circumcision for males. The

question arose in the early Christian community as to whether the Gentiles needed to follow the Judaic laws, or if they could become members of the Christian community without meeting these requirements. This led to the establishment of the above-mentioned guideline.)

II. INTOXICANTS AND GAMBLING

What does the Qur'an say regarding intoxicants and gambling?

> Qur'an: Say: "In wine and gambling is great sin and some profit, but the sin is greater than the profit" (Qur'an 2:219) Do not approach prayers with a befogged mind until you can understand all that you say (Qur'an 4:43). Intoxicants and gambling, (dedication of) stones, and (divination by) arrows are an abomination of Satan's handiwork. Eschew such (abomination), that you may prosper. Satan's plan is (but) to sow enmity and hatred between you, with intoxicants and gambling, and hinder you from the remembrance of God, and from prayer (5:90-91).

Opinions vary regarding the "degree of restriction" against drinking imposed by these verses. Some consider intoxicants totally prohibited, similar to pork; others feel that God's prohibition is not against drinking, but against getting drunk. They cite verse 4:43 to support their point. But some Hadeeth state that, when verses 5:90-91 were revealed, people broke containers of alcohol (for example: Tirmidhi 3649, Al-Muwatta 42.13). Here are some contradictory Hadeeth:

> Hadeeth: The prophet said: If people drink wine, flog them, if they drink again, flog them (again). And if they drink (wine again), kill them (Abu-Dawood 4467, 4469). Other Hadeeth mentioning floggings include Tirmidhi 3617. And Abu Dawood 4470 indicates that

the punishment of death for drinking was repealed. Someone informed Muhammad*, "In our country a special alcoholic drink called Al-Bit is prepared (for drinking)." The prophet said, "Every intoxicant is prohibited" (Bukhari 9.284).

Hadeeth: When an intoxicated man was found staggering, he grasped hold of the person who came to "arrest" him. When this was mentioned to the prophet, he laughed–but gave no command regarding (punishing) him (Abu Dawood 4461).

☞Ijtihad: How do we reconcile this apparent contradiction?

How does the Bible deal with intoxicants?
We have contradictory views between the Hebrew Scriptures/Old Testament and the New Testament:

Hebrew Scriptures/Old Testament: Be not among wine bibbers; among riotous eaters of flesh. For the drunkard and the glutton shall come to poverty; and drowsiness will cloth a man with rags. (Proverbs 23:20-21; 23: 29-35; 20:1). Old wine and new deprive my people of understanding (Hosea 4:11). Woe to those who demand strong drink as soon as they rise in the morning, and linger into the night while wine inflames them (Isaiah 5:11).
(Rabbi Magid's note: Bible and tradition forbid anything that could harm you physically).
(When they were isolated after the world was flooded), Lot's daughters got Lot drunk to have sex with him to have children. (Genesis 19:30-38).
(Rabbi Magid's note: The daughters assumed they were the only three people left on earth and that there would be no other man available to continue the human race).

New Testament: Jesus gave wine to his disciples to drink, calling it his blood (Matthew 26:26-30). Jesus drinks wine and eats (Luke 7:34-35). Jesus turns water to wine (John 2:1-11). Drink no longer water, but use a little wine for your stomach's sake and your infirmities (1 Timothy 5:23). And be not drunk with wine, wherein is excess; but be filled with the Spirit (Ephesians 5:18-19). Let us walk honestly, as in the day; not in rioting and drunkenness, not in chambering and wantonness, not in strife and envying (Romans 13:13). But I now write to you not to associate with anyone named brother, if he is immoral, greedy, an idolater, a slanderer, a drunkard, or a robber, not even to eat with such a person (1 Corinthians 5:11). Now the works of the flesh are obvious: immorality, impurity, idolatry, licentiousness, sorcery, hatreds, rivalry, jealousy, outbursts of fury, acts of selfishness, dissensions, factions, occasions of envy, drinking bouts, orgies, and the like (Galatians 5:19-20).

(Regina Pfeiffer's note: Wine is considered part of the needs of humanity in Sirach 39:26 stating that "chief of all needs for human life are water and fire, iron and salt, the heart of the wheat, milk, and honey, the blood of the grape, and oil and cloth." Moreover, Israel is compared to a vineyard, bearing good fruit when it adheres to the covenant. Wine is a symbolic image in both Hebrew and Christian Scriptures and is representative of God's care for the people. Excessive intoxication is also, particularly in Hebrew Scriptures/Old Testament, sometimes symbolic of the people's turning away from God. In one of the Scriptures accepted by certain but not all Christian communities as part of the Old Testament one finds this verse: "Wine is very life to man if taken in moderation. Does he really live who lacks the wine which was created for his joy? Joy of the heart, good cheer and merriment are wine drunk freely at the proper time. Headache, bitterness, and disgrace is wine drunk amid anger and strife. More and more wine is a snare; it lessens his strength and multiplies his wounds" (Sirach 31:27-30)

III. RIBA (Translated As Usury)

Doesn't Islam prohibit the giving and charging of interest on loans? I am not sure. While the Qur'an declares *riba* (usually translated as usury) as undesirable, it does not describe what constitutes usury:

> Qur'an: Do not gorge yourselves on usury, doubling it and redoubling it (Qur'an 3:130). Those who gorge themselves on usury will be like those whom the Evil One has driven to madness. That is because they say: "Trade is like usury but God has permitted trade and forbidden usury." God will deprive (those who practice) usury of all blessing, but will (on the other hand) bless deeds of charity: . . . O you who believe! Fear God and give up what remains of your demand for usury, if you are indeed believers. If you repent, you shall be entitled to (a return of) your capital sums. . . . If the debtor is in difficulty, grant him time till it is easy for him to repay (the loan). But if you remit it by way of charity, that is best for you. . . . (Qur'an 2:275-280). Whatever you may give out in usury, so that it might increase through (other) people's possessions, (it) will bring (you) no increase in the sight of God–whereas all that you give out in charity, seeking God's countenance (will be blessed by him) (Qur'an 30:39).

As we see, the only definition we have of usury is in Qur'anic verse 3:130 ("doubling and redoubling") and indirectly in verse 2:279 ("you shall be entitled to a return of your capital"). Unfortunately, Muhammad* died without explaining what constitutes usury.

Hadeeth: Thus, Umar stated, "I wish God's Apostle had not left us before giving us a definite verdict on . . . the various types of usury" (Bukhari 7.493).

The prophet gave the following varied examples of usury:

(A) Bartering of commodities, except if it is from hand to hand (i.e., on the spot) and equal in amount (Bukhari 3.294, 3.344, 3.379, 3.382). (B) Exchanging an inferior item for one of superior quality. You should sell the first and then buy the second (Bukhari 3.405, 3.499, 3.506). (C) Exchanging unequal weights of items (Al Muwatta 3128). (D) Bartering dry dates for fresh dates is usury, except for home consumption (Muslim 3687). (E) Gold is to be paid for by gold, silver by silver, wheat by wheat, barley by barley, dates by dates, salt by salt, like by like, payment being made hand to hand. He who makes an addition to it, or asks for an addition, deals in usury. The receiver and the giver are equally guilty (Muslim 3854). (F) "Unlike" type transactions can be acceptable if payment is made on the spot (Abu Dawood 3343; Muslim 3856). (G) Combining two transactions into one would be usurious (Abu Dawood 3454). (H) "All claims to usury of the pre-Islamic period have been abolished. You shall have your capital sums. Deal not unjustly and you shall not be dealt with unjustly" (Abu Dawood 3328). (I) "If somebody owes you something and he sends you a present of a load of chopped straw, barley, or provender, do not take it, as it is usury" (Bukhari 5.159), (J) "If anyone intercedes for his brother and he (the latter) presents a gift to him (the former) for it and he accepts it, he approaches usury" (Abu Dawood 3534). (K) "The most prevalent kind of usury is going to lengths in talking unjustly against a Muslim's honor" (Abu Dawood 4858).

Let us consider these a little more in depth:

(1) Examining the Qur'anic verses:
(I) Verse 3:130 clarifies that a transaction is usurious if the amount "doubles and redoubles"–possibly in a short time period. If the interest charged is 5% compounding annually, the amount due will double in about 15 years. Is this usury?
(II) Verse 2:279 states that the creditor shall be entitled to a return of his principal sum. However, since inflation did not exist 1,400 years ago, its discussion in the Qur'an would have been unintelligible to people then. But today, inflation is an economic reality. For example, if A loaned B $100,000 to buy a home 30 years back, with the amount to be repaid now, should B still repay only $100,000–even though the purchasing power of today's $100,000 would probably equal only $20,000 in terms of "1970 dollars"?

☛ Ijithad: Shouldn't the phrase "return of capital" mean return of the money borrowed in terms of their value at the time of borrowing? In the above example then, shouldn't B pay back his creditor $500,000 instead of $100,000 that he borrowed 30 years back (assuming this represented the inflation rate)?

(2) Examining Hadeeth:
(I) We see in Hadeeth G-H that both "like-kind" and "unlike- kind" barters could be acceptable if the trade is "on the spot." Then, will "forward trading," as happens with many agricultural commodities (such as cotton, rice, wheat, etc.), be deemed usurious?
(II) I find the implications of Hadeeth I-K to be beautiful and broad-based. They underscore that taking undue advantage of anyone's unfortunate situation would be usurious. Thus, shouldn't commercial gifts and bribes be considered usury and be totally unacceptable?

What about "interest-free banking/profit-and-loss schemes (PLS)?"
It is generally believed that receiving or giving a fixed rate of return on a loan would be usury; but not if the loaned money is "at risk" [for example by the lender also being involved in the business].

☞ Ijtihad: How will you establish a "profit-and-loss" repayment schedule on a loan for personal reasons (such as marriage)?

☞ Ijtihad: What should a 65-year-old widow do with the money her husband left her? Under the bank's fixed-deposit scheme, she is happy with the guaranteed income she receives. Will it be "Islamic" to force her to put her money in PLS–and possibly lose everything?

☞ Ijtihad: How will the profit-and-loss system deal with bankruptcy?

☞ Ijtihad: If a person can either invest his limited money in a business or give it as a loan, will he not be justified in asking the debtor to give him the rate of return prevailing in the banking system? How many people have unlimited cash lying around to give as interest-free loans?

Is the demand for interest-free banking impacting business practices?
Yes. Pakistan's Supreme Court declared interest-bearing bank accounts un-Islamic and gave the government up to June 2001 to change the system. On appeal, the government now has up to June 30, 2002, to implement this change.

☞ Ijtihad: Can any government say to the World Bank and Asian Development Bank that it cannot pay fixed interest but still wants loans? Has even Saudi Arabia implemented interest-free banking?

☞ Ijtihad: As a first step, shouldn't we first have an objective (not emotional) discussion on what constitutes riba?

Saleem, what do you feel should be the bottom line on riba?
People should not take undue advantage of anyone's predicament, be it financial, social, psychological, or medical. That would be *riba*. For example, asking for or accepting bribes to give a phone connection, issue a passport, provide a license, or reduce the utilities bill, etc. should be labeled as *riba*. Also, will it not be *riba* for a trader, who normally sells rice or fertilizer for $10 per bag, to charge $20 because of shortage (assuming his cost had not changed)?

Personal note: In 1955, when I was 15, I was among the 20 Boy Scouts selected to represent Pakistan at the 8ᵗʰ World Boy Scouts Jamboree held in Canada. About a week before our tickets were to be purchased, the Pakistani government devalued its currency. Thus, I was asked to pay Rs. 1,000 [then about $250–a large sum in terms of purchasing power] toward the ticket cost. My mother, a recent widow, did not have this money. But, like any other loving mother, she wanted me to go. So she took me to our neighbor in Karachi, a Parsee (Zoroastrian) gentleman, Mr. Daver, and tearfully asked if he could loan us the money. That loving man not only did so, but said, "Saleem, I am loaning this money to you, not to your mother. You repay it whenever you start earning; there is no deadline for repayment. I don't need any interest, just the principal. And congratulations!" It was ten years later (1965) when I started earning money. Even then, it took me about a year to repay the loan in full. Mr. Daver was in no hurry–only happy that I was fulfilling the obligation. That trip, of course, opened my eyes to the world. May God bless Mr. Daver and his family. While Mr. Daver's gesture is an excellent example of an interest-free loan, how many people can provide such loans for 10+ years?

☛ Ijtihad: How would "interest-free banking" or "profit-and-loss account" deal with the above-mentioned situation?

☛ Ijtihad: Many God-fearing Muslims leave large sums in bank "interest-free" checking accounts in the West. The bankers like this and, in accordance with normal banking practices, use these funds to make significant profits (possibly running into millions of dollars annually). Couldn't these God-fearing Muslims put the same money in interest-earning accounts instead and use the proceeds for charity? After all, Qur'anic verse 2:276 states "God will deprive usury of all blessing, but will give increase for deeds of charity."

What does the Bible say about usury?

> The Hebrew Scriptures/Old Testament: The person who sins, only he shall die. Thus, if a man is righteous

and does what is just and right . . . If he has not lent at advance interest or exacted accrued interest . . . such a man shall live (Ezekiel 18: 4-9). If you lend money to one of your poor neighbors among My people, you shall not act like an extortioner toward him by demanding interest from him. If you take your neighbor's cloak as a pledge, you shall return it to him before sunset (Exodus 22:24-25). You shall not demand interest from your countrymen on a loan of money or of food or of anything else on which interest is usually demanded. You may demand interest from a foreigner, but not from your countryman (Exodus 22:2425).

(Rabbi Magid's note: There is a vast difference between interest on a loan and usury, which is defined in English as interest beyond what is customary and usual).

The New Testament: I could not find any passage on the subject.

☛ Ijtihad: Since we do not find *riba* defined, either in the Qur'an or Hadeeth, as charging interest on loans–but find that charging interest on loans is unacceptable in the Hebrew Scriptures/Old Testament–isn't it possible that devout Muslims, who initially linked *riba* with interest, may have based it on the Jewish practice that may have been prevalent in Arabia and elsewhere at that time? Even in the Jewish case, isn't there a difference between interest on loan and usury (as clarified by Rabbi Magid above)?

☛ Ijtihad: Since neither the Qur'an nor Hadeeth define what is *riba*, shouldn't we follow the Qur'anic injunction "Let there be no compulsion in religion" (Qur'an 2:256) and let individuals, organizations, and governments decide how they should invest money–as long as they are given choices?

CHAPTER 11. SLAVERY AND ORPHANS

I. SLAVERY

Isn't it true that the Qur'an permits men to have many slave girls?
Regarding slaves–male and female–God commands as follows:

> Qur'an: It is not righteousness that you turn your faces
> toward East or West; but it is righteousness to believe
> in God, the Last Day, the Angels, the Book, and the
> Messengers; to spend of your substance out of love for
> Him for your kin, for orphans, for the needy, for the
> wayfarer, for those who ask, and for the ransom of
> slaves; to be steadfast in prayer and practice regular
> charity; to fulfil the contracts which you have made;
> and to be firm and patient in pain (or suffering) and
> adversity, and throughout all periods of panic (Qur'an
> 2:177; see also Qur'an 4:6, 4:36).

Turning the face east or west refers to the direction faced (the Ka'bah)
while praying. Thus, all above-mentioned actions, including the freeing
of slaves, are more righteous than "empty prayers."

> Qur'an: Marry those among you who are single or the
> virtuous ones among your slaves, male or female. . .
> (Qur'an 24:32).

*But isn't it true that Muslim men can have any number of slaves and
therefore an unlimited number of "mistresses" in the harem?*
No. In fact, we do not even find the word "harem" in either the Qur'an
or Hadeeth. As we saw in Chapter 8, marrying up to four women is
permitted, primarily to provide protection and support to destitute
women and children.

But what about slave girls being forced into prostitution?

> Qur'an: You are forbidden to inherit women against
> their will (Qur'an 4:19). . . . Do not force your maids to
> prostitution when they desire chastity (Qur'an 24:33).

Does the Qur'an allow women to have male slaves?
Yes. And women can also marry their male slaves:

> Qur'an: Marry those among you who are single or the
> virtuous ones among your slaves, male or female. . .
> (Qur'an 24:32).

Women were also allowed to appear freely before their male slaves but
were reminded of God's omnipresence.

> Qur'an: There is no blame (on these women if they
> appear) before . . . the (slaves) whom their right hands
> possess. (Qur'an 33.55; also: 24.31).

Could slaves, male or female, dream of freedom?
Yes. Muslims were encouraged to free slaves, and slaves were
encouraged to strive to "earn" their freedom.

> Qur'an: If slaves ask for a deed in writing (to enable
> them to earn their freedom for a certain sum), give
> them such a deed, if you know any good in them.
> Indeed, also give them something yourselves out of the
> means which God has given to you (24:33).

*How do the Hebrew Scriptures/Old Testament and New Testament
deal with slavery, especially female slavery, and forced marriage?*

> Hebrew Scriptures/Old Testament: When you go to
> war against your enemies, and the Lord your God has
> delivered them to your hands and you have taken them

captive, and you see among the captives a beautiful woman and you desire to make her your wife, then you shall bring her to your home, and she shall shave her head and pare her nails; and she shall put the raiment of her captivity from off her, and shall remain in your house and bewail her father and mother a full month: and after that you shall go in unto her, and be her husband and she, your wife (Deuteronomy 21:10-13). Solomon enslaved the Hittites, Amorites, Perizzites, Hivitites, and Jebusites, and their children continued to be enslaved by the Hebrews for generations (2 Chronicles 8:7-8). Things the earth cannot bear: A slave to become a ruler (Proverbs 30:21-22). . . . At the end of every seven years, free any Hebrew you hold as slave (Jeremiah 34:14).

(Rabbi Magid's note: In discussing the above-mentioned passages, we must keep in mind the time frame and context involved. Also, there were different categories of slaves. Finally, even Biblical "slavery" was vastly different from slavery of the American Civil War era. The laws regarding work and the Sabbath applied even to "slaves," who were actually part of the family in many respects).

New Testament: The disciple is not above his master, nor is the slave above his lord (Matthew 10:24).

II. ORPHANS

How are orphans to be treated?
They are to be treated with the utmost justice, compassion, and sincerity. God makes it clear that those managing the properties of orphans should carry out their fiduciary responsibilities with the utmost care; Hadeeth also underscore this point:

Qur'an: To orphans restore their property (when they reach their age), nor substitute (your) worthless things for (their) good ones; and devour not their substance (by mixing it up) with your own (Qur'an 4:2). Make a trial of orphans until they reach the age of marriage; if then you find sound judgment in them, release their property to them; but do not consume it wastefully nor in haste against their growing up. If the guardian is well-off, let him claim no remuneration; but if he is poor, let him have for himself what is just and reasonable. When you release their property to them, take witnesses in their presence (Qur'an 4:6). Let those (disposing of an estate) have the same fear in their minds as they would have for their own if they had left a helpless family behind (Qur'an 4: 9). Those who unjustly eat up the property of orphans, eat up a fire into their own bodies: they will soon be enduring a blazing fire (Qur'an 4:10). Come not nigh to the orphan's property except to improve it (Qur'an 6: 152; 17:34). (Also see Qur'an 17:34, 89:17).

Hadeeth: Muhammad* explained that the best thing to do is what is for their (orphans') good; if you mix their affairs with yours, they are your brethren (Abu Dawood 2865).

CHAPTER 12. AMUSEMENT, MUSIC, DANCE, AND CULTURE

Doesn't Islam prohibit all forms of amusement?
No. I could not find any passage in the Qur'an which prohibits, or even indirectly hints at a dislike of, amusement and entertainment so long as these are not directed at lust, greed, materialism, and other evils. Generally, unless something has been prohibited and/or made illegal, it is accepted and lawful.

> Qur'an: Do not make unlawful the good things which God has made lawful for you, but commit no transgression (5:87).

> Hadeeth: Muhammad* said, "I have been sent with an easy and straightforward religion" (Fiqh-us-Sunnah, 2:153). "...So do not be extremists..." (Bukhari 1:38).

I. RELAXATION, ENTERTAINMENT, DANCE, AND MUSIC

A. Relaxation: Muhammad* declared, "The days of Eid celebration . . . are days of eating and drinking (non-alcoholic drinks) and of remembering God, the Exalted." (Fiqh us Sunnah 2.153; Bukhari 2.70, 2.72, 5.268).

B. Dance: The prophet took Aisha to watch some African Muslims celebrate the festival of Eid by singing and dancing with spears (Bukhari 4.730, 7.163, Fiqh-us-Sunnah 2.153, Tirmidhi 6040). In another case, a woman came to the prophet and said: "Apostle of God,

I have taken a vow to play the tambourine for you." He responded, "Fulfil your vow" (Abu Dawood 3306).

C. Entertainment: Someone asked the prophet: "If someone provides me no entertainment or hospitality, shall I provide him entertainment? He replied, "Yes" (Al-Tirmidhi 4248; similar report: Abu Dawood 3742).

D. Amusement: The prophet suggested that there should be entertainment (singing, playing the tambourine, etc.) at weddings (Bukhari 7.92A, 4.730, 7.163; Fiqh-us-Sunnah 2.153; Tirmidhi 3152, 6040). Thus, he liked singing and tambourine playing at his own wedding (Bukhari 5.336).

E. Bells: Muhammad* said: "The bell is the musical instrument of Satan" (Muslim 5279). Note: In what context he stated this is unclear since this concept goes counter to other Hadeeth dealing with music.

II. POETRY

F. Muhammad* recited poetry while helping others dig a trench (Bukhari 5.432) and build a mosque (Bukhari 5.245). Once he asked a companion to keep on reciting the work of a particular poet till he had recited "one hundred couplets" (Muslim 5602). At another time, the prophet appreciated the Huda (songs sung in harmony with the camel's walk) sung by a camel-driver, Amir (Bukhari 9.29, 8.343, 8.169, 5.509). Among Muhammad's* companions who also recited poetry were Abu Bakar (Bukhari 7.558, 7.581), Hasan (Muhammad's* grandson) (Bukhari 5.467, 4.731), and Abu Hurayra (Bukhari 3.707). Aisha was not only knowledgeable about religion but also medicine and also was a gifted poetess. Muhammad* suggested to his followers to "learn your religion from this red-colored lady" (perhaps she was a redhead?) (Biography of Aisha bint Abi Bakar in Alim, 1986).

G. Muhammad* stated, "In eloquence, there is magic; in knowledge, ignorance; in poetry, wisdom; and in speech, heaviness" (Abu Dawood 4994; also: Bukhari 8.166). He also asserted, "The believer strives with his sword and his tongue" (Tirmidhi 4795) and clarified that poetry ". . . is speech. What is good in it is good, and what is bad is bad" (Tirmidhi 4807). Poetry which contains wisdom, praises of Islam, or encouragement of piety would be appreciated; conversely, that which ridicules Muslims or praises wrongdoers or lewdness would be prohibited (Fiqh-us-Sunnah 2.72, Bukhari 4.434; also Muslim 5610, 5611; Bukhari 8.175, 8.176; Al-Muwatta 9.96).

III. PLAYING WITH DOLLS

H. Once when the prophet saw Aisha playing with her dolls, he asked, "What is this?" She replied: "My dolls." Among them, he saw a horse with wings made of rags and asked: "What is this?" She replied: "A horse." He asked: "What is this it has on it?" She replied: "Two wings." He asked: "A horse with two wings?" She replied: "Have you not heard that Solomon had horses with wings?" Thereupon the apostle laughed so heartily that Aisha could see his molar teeth (Abu Dawood 4914). Aisha would often invite her friends to play with her dolls. And if any of them would hide away when the prophet returned home, he would call them to join and play with Aisha (Fateh-al-Bari page 143, Vol.13; Bukhari 8.151).

IV. HORSE RACING

I. Once Muhammad* arranged for a horse race (Bukhari 4.120, 9.436). The prophet advised: "There must be no shouting or leading another's horse to one's side." Yahya the narrator added this was when racing was for a wager. (Abu Dawood 2575).

V. STATUES AND CHURCHES

J. It is permissible to pray inside church: Some companions prayed in churches, except for churches with statues or sculptures (Fiqh-us-Sunnah 2.75).

☛Ijtihad: What forms of entertainment are <u>not</u> acceptable in Islam? Wouldn't setting strict limits conflict with the Qur'anic injunction that there should be no compulsion in religion? Isn't Islam "an easy religion"?

How does the Bible treat the subject of music, dancing, poetry, and other forms of amusement and entertainment?
There seems to be no prohibition against such entertainment in either Scripture.

CHAPTER 13 PUNISHMENT FOR CRIMES DURING ONE'S LIFE; REWARD & PUNISHMENT IN THE HEREAFTER

I. PUNISHMENT FOR CRIMES IN THIS LIFE

Doesn't the Qur'an enjoin "an eye for an eye and a tooth for a tooth" in retaliatory punishment?
No. That is in the Hebrew Scriptures/Old Testament; the Qur'an adds "it is better to forgive." The New Testament suggests "turning the other cheek."

> Hebrew Scriptures/Old Testament: If anyone kills any human being, he shall be put to death. One who kills a beast shall make restitution for it: life for life. If anyone maims his fellow, as he has done so shall it be done to him: fracture for fracture, eye for eye, tooth for tooth. The injury he inflicted on another shall be inflicted on him. One who kills a beast shall make restitution for it; but anyone who kills a human shall be put to death (Leviticus 24:17-21).
> (Rabbi Magid's note: There never was an actual policy of having your tooth removed for knocking out someone's tooth; rather, it was always understood as financial restitution.)

> New Testament: You have heard that it has been said, An eye for an eye, a tooth for a tooth. But I say unto you, That you resist not evil: but whoever shall smite you on your cheek, turn to him the other also. And if a man will sue you at the law and take away your coat, let him have your cloak also. And whosoever shall

compel you to go a mile, go with him two. Give to him
that asks you, and from him that would borrow of you,
do not turn him away (Matthew:38-42).

Qur'an: We ordained therein for them: "Life for life,
eye for eye, nose for nose, ear for ear, tooth for tooth,
and wounds equal for equal." But, if anyone remits the
retaliation by way of charity, it is an act of atonement
for himself . . . (Qur'an 5:45). The law of equality is
prescribed to you in cases of murder: the free for the
free, the slave for the slave, the woman for the woman.
But if any remission is made by the brother of the slain,
then grant any reasonable demand and compensate him
with handsome gratitude (Qur'an 2:178). And the
recompense for an injury is an injury equal thereto (in
degree): but if a person forgives and makes
reconciliation, His reward is due from God (Qur'an
42:40).
Hadeeth: A murderer was brought before the prophet.
The prophet asked the victim's legal guardian: "Do you
forgive him?" He said: "No." "Will you accept blood-
money?" "No." "Will you kill him?" "Yes." The
prophet said: "Take him away." After repeating this line
of inquiry four times, the prophet said: "If you forgive
him, he will bear the burden of his own sins and the sins
of the victim." The guardian then forgave him (Abu
Dawood 4484).

Are hands of thieves are to be cut off?

Qur'an: As to the thief, male or female, cut off his or
her hands: a punishment by way of example from God
for their crime. . . . But if the thief repents after his
crime and amends his conduct, God turns to him in
forgiveness (Qur'an 5:38-9).

As indicated above, the party who was robbed could forgive the thief and save him from having his hand cut off.

Can even hands of a petty thief, who steals because of hunger, be cut?
No. Different Hadeeth stipulate different "minimum" values of the stolen goods for the hand to be cut off. For example:

> Hadeeth: A person was punished for theft valued at a quarter dinar (Al-Muwatta 41.27). Another person was pardoned for a 60 dirham theft (Al-Muwatta 41.33). [Dinar and dirham are currency units. See Glossary].

We don't have details to explain this difference. It does follow, however, that petty thieves and those who steal out of necessity should not receive punishment. But corrupt officials and rulers, who steal and/or accept bribes out of greed, should.

What punishment for theft is prescribed in the Bible?

> Hebrew Scriptures/Old Testament: When a man steals an ox or a sheep and slaughters or sells it, he shall restore five oxen for the one ox, and four sheep for the one sheep (Exodus 21:37). If a thief is caught in the act of housebreaking and beaten to death, there is no bloodguilt involved. But, if after sunrise he is thus beaten, there is bloodguilt. He must make full restitution. If he has nothing, he shall be sold to pay for his theft. If what he stole is found alive in his possession, be it an ox, an ass, or a sheep, he shall restore two animals for each one stolen (Exodus 22:1-3).
> (Rabbi Magid's note: By 2,000 years ago, this [system] was changed to one of restitution).

II. REWARD AND PUNISHMENT IN THE HEREAFTER

1. Death and Rebirth

How does the Qur'an look upon death?
As a natural process, from which no human–or any other living matter–can escape:

> Qur'an: Every soul shall have a taste of death: in the end to Us shall you be brought back (Qur'an 29:57).

Among His 99 attributes (Appendix), God is described not only as "Khaliq" (Creator of Life) but also as "Mumit" (Creator of Death). Thus, at the end of life, we "graduate" into our new "life"–in death. And since that "life" is eternal, many Muslim Sufis have described our current life to be a dream, from which we will "wake up" in death.

And what are the Qur'an's views on reincarnation?

> Qur'an: We have decreed death to be your common lot, and We are not to be frustrated from changing your forms and creating you (again) in (forms) that you do not know (Qur'an 56:60-61).

☞ Ijtihad: Doesn't this suggest reincarnation?

How does the Bible look upon death and reincarnation?

> Hebrew Scriptures/Old Testament: Everyone will die because of his own sins (Jeremiah 31:30). The soul that sins shall die (Ezekiel 18:4). When a righteous person turns away from his own righteousness and does wrong, he shall die for it; he shall die for the wrong he has done (Ezekiel 18:26). A season is set for everything, a time for every experience under the

heaven: A time for being born and a time for dying
(Ecclesiastes 3:1-2)
(Rabbi Magid's note: In general, the Hebrew Scriptures
/Old Testament makes no direct causal relationship
between sin and death. In fact, the Psalms raise the
question as to why evil seems to prosper. Judaism sees
death as inevitable and part of life.)
(Regina Pfeiffer's note: It could be added here that long
life was seen as a blessing from God, indicative of a
person who had lived a righteous life. However, the
book of Job is one that challenges that perspective
regarding the connection between long life and
righteousness.)

New Testament: Unless you repent, you shall all perish
(Luke 13:1-5). For if you live after the flesh, you will
die; but if you through the Spirit do mortify the deeds
of the body, you shall live (Romans 8:13). And as it is
appointed unto men once to die, but after this is the
judgment: So Christ was once offered to bear the sins
of many; and unto them who look for him shall he
appear the second time without sin unto salvation
(Hebrews 9:27-28).
(Regina Pfeiffer's note: In the Christian Scriptures,
death is correlated more with the concept of sin. A key
idea of the Christian Scriptures, which is a later
development within Judaism, is the concept of the
resurrection of the body with the coming of the
Messiah. Therefore, death is seen as death of the body,
but not the spirit.)

Reincarnation: I do not recall any Biblical passage
dealing with this subject.
(Rabbi Magid's note: Reincarnation is not part of
Biblical tradition.)

(Regina Pfeiffer's note: Reincarnation is not a doctrine of the Judaic or Christian faith. Elijah is a prophet who was taken to heaven in a fiery chariot (See 2 Kings 2:1-11). It was believed among those who awaited the Messiah that Elijah would precede the coming of the Messiah (see Malachi 3:23. But he would appear as Elijah back from the dead not as another, newly incarnated version of Elijah.)

2. Reward and Punishment in the Hereafter

Isn't it true that, according to the Qur'an, men will have virgin women in paradise as a reward for virtuous living?
Some people might get disappointed! The Qur'an states that the righteous will have "hoor" for companions. But who are "hoors'? No details are provided, other than they are "companions with large eyes." "Hoor" should thus be taken as another technical term, whose meaning remains unclear, similar to terms such as angels and jinns. We have the following general description of Paradise:

> Qur'an: The righteous will be in gardens and in happiness, enjoying the (bliss) which their Lord has bestowed on them; and their Lord shall deliver them from the penalty of the fire. (To them will be said) "Eat and drink with profit and health because of your (good) deeds." They will recline (with ease) on thrones (of dignity), arranged in ranks; and We shall join them to companions with beautiful big and lustrous eyes. And those who believe and whose families follow them in Faith, to them shall We join their families: nor shall We deprive them (of the fruit) of their works: (Yet) is each individual in pledge for his deeds. And We shall bestow on them of fruit and meat–anything they shall desire. They shall there exchange one with another a (loving) cup free of frivolity, free of all taint of ill. Round about

them will serve (devoted) youths, (handsome) as pearls well-guarded. They will advance to each other engaging in mutual enquiry (52:17-25). (See also Qur'an 56:10-26).

And what does the Qur'an say about punishment in hell?

Qur'an: . . . We have truly made it (Tree of Zuqqum) (as) a trial for the wrongdoers. For it is a tree that springs out of the bottom of Hell Fire: The shoots of its fruit-stalks are like the heads of devils: Truly they will eat thereof and fill their bellies therewith. Then, on top of that, they will be given a mixture made of boiling water. Then shall their return be to the (Blazing) Fire (Qur'an 37.62-68. Also, see Qur'an 22:19-21). [Note: The "Tree of Zuqqum" is another undefined technical term.]

How does the Bible describe reward and punishment in the afterlife?

Hebrew Scriptures/Old Testament:
There is no discussion of the afterlife in the Hebrew Scriptures/Old Testament; neither of any reward or punishment after we die.
(Rabbi Magid's note: This is an incredibly complex subject.)

New Testament: The New Testament talks about "everlasting happiness" and "hellfire." Beyond these, however, there is no description of what it will be "like" in these places.
(Regina Pfeiffer's note: There is no description of heaven as a particular place. Instead, heaven is the dwelling place of the Lord, the presence of God, not as a place, but as a sense of divine transcendence. Heaven

could also be used as a veiled expression for God instead of saying God's name. Early Judaism called the abode of the dead "Scheol". It gradually developed from the image of a dark, colorless place over which God has dominion but in which its inhabitants had no remembrance of nor praise for God. Later Judaism developed the idea that it was a place in which the dead remained to await judgment and resurrection. "Gehenna", another term used in both Hebrew and Christian Scriptures, later becomes the image in apocalyptic literature (a style of writing that emphasizes the final struggle between good and evil with good prevailing) of the place of eternal torment for the impious after their death and "eschaton" (end times –when the Messiah comes). It is used in this sense particularly in the Christian Scriptures.

CHAPTER 14. INTROSPECTIVE ANALYSIS

Can you summarize what have we learned so far about Islamic teachings and Muslim practices?
Islamic teachings: God's religion will always exist. Brought to us through numerous prophets that He sent the world over across several thousand years, God's message is simple: Believe in Him and lead a righteous life. In the future, God may continue to send reformers–to earth and to other planets to which humanity may expand in the future–to redirect our "derailed" energy onto the right path. Being disillusioned with the hollowness and dogmatism of various divisive ritualistic religious practices, humans have, in the recent past, turned increasingly to the "god" of materialism. However, finding that to be shallow, they are earnestly yearning for spirituality and "intellectual connection" with God: a connection which replaces "them versus us" with "all of us together"; "the only path" with "various paths"; and "the only prophet" with "all God's prophets." As humans rise to higher intellectual levels, I believe that Islam, as defined in this book, will attract more followers.

Muslim practices: Consider the following incident: It was mid-October, 2001. A month had passed since the September 11th tragedy. My six-session class at the University of Hawaii on *Understanding Islam* was half completed. A young man, disturbed by the Taliban's defiant attitude in Afghanistan, asked: "Saleem, wouldn't the world have been a better place had Muhammad not been born?"

I was struck by lightening. How could anyone speak this way of the prophet*? Then I realized that we had entirely different reference points: while mine was based on the <u>teachings</u> of Islam as laid down in the Qur'an, his was based on the <u>practices</u> of some Muslims, exemplified by the September 11th tragedy and other questionable acts referred to in this book. Isn't it ironic, I thought, that while the Qur'an enjoins Muslims to send prayers of peace for Muhammad* and the other prophets* (hence we add "peace be upon him" every time we mention a prophet's name), the actions of some Muslims might be resulting in people sending Muhammad* curses!

How did you respond?
That day, we discussed Qur'anic injunctions on some women-related issues such as dress code, marriage and divorce, etc. (summarized in Chapters 7, 8, and 9). When we compared these with pre-Islamic practices and Biblical injunctions, the class agreed that Muhammad had indeed brought about many reforms in the society. We also agreed that perhaps these reforms are being followed more closely today by non-Muslims than Muslims.

Can you give examples of what do you mean?
In their desire to abide strictly by Muslim teachings, some devout Muslims seem to draw practically all their guidance from Hadeeth. And while many Hadeeth complement the Qur'an, others, as we saw in Chapter 3 and elsewhere in this document, do not appear to do so.

From where may Muhammad* have obtained guidance on any issue prior to receiving revelation from God on that issue?
On matters of theology and principles, such as unity of God and universality of His message, Muhammad* undoubtedly depended entirely on guidance from the Creator. But on matters dealing with everyday issues, such as interpersonal relations, isn't it possible that, in some cases, he also may have relied on the Jewish and Christian traditions? After all, all three religions spring from the same source: the prophet Abraham*. Thus, if we find some Hadeeth to be closer to Hebrew Scriptures/Old Testament or New Testament passages than to the Qur'an, can we not conclude that these Hadeeth probably pedate Qur'anic revelations on those subjects? Examples such as punishment for adultery, veiling of women, rights of women, laws of inheritance, dietary restrictions, usury, and religious violence are discussed in various chapters of this book.

But nowadays, haven't Jews and Christians stopped following some questionable Biblical passages dealing with interpersonal issues?
That is right. In his Foreword, Gregg Kinkley reminds us "not to judge Judaism by what the Torah seems to say in one or two verses quoted herein as the full reach of Jewish law encompassing the full range of human interaction. Jewish law was forced long ago to draw deeply from other wells, all as inspired as the original springs of the Torah itself." And Regina Pfeiffer's Foreword adds, "Although Dr. Ahmed quotes passages from the Bible that address the questions he raises, one caveat must be noted: all three traditions are conditioned by the specific time, place and people out of which they developed. Each must seek continually for answers that renew and challenge, invite and inspire, seek and find peace for its adherents in the world of today."

So, in many instances, Jews and Christians have <u>dropped</u> or modified practices enjoined in their sacred texts. For example, Jews do not go about stoning adulterers to death anymore (although this is prescribed in Leviticus 20:10)and Christian men do not require Christian women to be veiled or be subservient to men anymore (although this is prescribed in 1 Corinthians 11:4-9).

And what have Muslims done?
They seem to have <u>picked up</u> what Jews and Christians discarded! How? By following some Hadeeth—which seem to be based on Biblical injunctions—at the expense of perfectly fine Qur'anic injunctions modifying them. How could this have happened? We can probably put the blame on the unquestioned following of Hadeeth, without pausing to reflect whether these could have predated Qur'anic revelations on those subjects. How insidious this has become may perhaps be gleaned by the following explanation in footnote No. 2954 to the Qur'anic verses 24:2-3 in Abdullah Yusuf Ali's translation of the Qur'an (Ali 1989, page 865). While these verses state, in no uncertain terms, that those guilty of adultery or fornication (*zina*) are to be flogged with 100 stripes and thereafter permitted to marry only others similarly guilty (which means they should survive the punishment), the explanation within brackets in the footnote states: "Although *zina* covers both

adultery and fornication, in the opinion of Muslim jurists, the punishment laid down here applies only to unmarried persons. As for married persons, their punishment, according to the Sunnah of the prophet (peace be upon him), is stoning to death." So, Muslims are modifying their sacred text by a human compilation, rather than discarding the latter whenever it seems to contradict with the former! Another sad fact is that Abdullah Yusuf Ali's original translation (published in 1935) did not have this footnote; it was added later by those who revised his translation.

But doesn't God declare the Qur'an to be "a Tablet preserved"?
That is correct. And, as God has promised in the Qur'an, it should remain as such. By adding potentially tangential material, as the one quoted above, I fear we may be doing irreversible damage to the spirit of that Book. In contrast, let us also remember that the collection of Hadeeth is not "perfect." Please recall that, because he apprehended that people might tamper with his teachings and actions, Muhammad* had declared:

> Hadeeth: "Whoever revives a Sunnah which dies after me will be rewarded in the Hereafter; and whoever introduces some evil innovation, which was not approved by God or His messenger, will be punished" (Tirmidhi 168).

Can you cite some differences between Qur'anic injunctions and current Muslim practices?
Based on my reading of the Qur'an, listed below are some troubling questions regarding some Muslim practices that come to my mind:

1. Since the Qur'an declares "Let there be no compulsion in religion" (Qur'an 2:256), why should some Muslim countries prohibit missionary activities by followers of other religions?

2. Since the Qur'an urges: "Invite others to the way of your Lord with wisdom and beautiful preaching (Qur'an 16:125)" why do we

have to become emotional and argumentative when discussing religion? Why should we adopt an antagonistic attitude toward other religions rather than befriending their followers? Why do some Muslims call Christians and Jews as "infidels" when the Qur'an declares them to be "People of the Book"?

3. Since the Qur'an defines jihad as a struggle for righteousness and defense of religion against oppressors (Qur'an 2:190-3), why do some Muslim rulers label their own aggressive designs–even wars with other Muslim countries–as jihad? Where does the Qur'an permit killing innocent non-Muslims in our quest for realizing political goals–howsoever justified we feel these goals might be?

4. Since Qur'an asks men and women to be modestly dressed with women also covering their bosoms (Qur'an 24:30-31), why do some Muslim societies require women to be completely veiled?

5. Since the Qur'an affirms equality and reciprocity of sexes–why are women in some Muslim societies denied education, restricted in the types of jobs they can do, and placed completely at the mercy of their husbands and/or other male family members? Especially when they might be more intelligent than their male counterparts? Why are they are forced into marriage, divorced at the whim of their husbands, and have virtually no recourse to justice when accused falsely of any crime?

6. Since Muhammad* advised: Avoid inflicting the prescribed penalty on Muslims as much as you can, and if there is any way out, let a man go. For it is better for a leader to make a mistake in forgiving than to make a mistake in punishing (Tirmidhi 3570), shouldn't we show leniency in prescribing punishment for human failings?

7. Since the Qur'an places the utmost emphasis on righteousness as the foundation of the religion and declares that the only ranking among humans in the sight of God is in the degree of our

righteousness (Qur'an 49:13), why do some Muslims look upon the so-called Five Pillars of Islam as the most important duties for Muslims? Are not kindness to others, honesty, hard work, and discipline, etc., more important than empty prayers and fasting?

8.   Since the Qur'an permits eating even pork in case of necessity (Qur'an 2:172-3), do we need to make "halal" meat an issue? Doesn't the fact that in western countries animals are slaughtered en-masse and mechanically, coupled with the prophets* advised to say "Bismillah" over food and eat it, suffice?

9.   Do we need to make *riba* ("usury") an issue when neither the Qur.an nor Hadeeth define what constitutes *riba/*? How do we cope with the impact of inflation in long-term loans if we do not permit creditors to charge interest at least to keep up with inflation? And while the issue remains unresolved, couldn't devout Muslims, who keep billions of dollars in non-interest bearing accounts in the West, place this in interest-bearing accounts instead and give in charity the millions earned in interest?

10. Since the Qur'an directs Muslims to conduct their affairs by mutual consultation (Qur'an 42:38), shouldn't we encourage the establishment of democratic processes at all levels? Shouldn't we stop issuing "fatwas" (religious edicts) on mere emotionalism, anger, and impatience without consulting others?

11. Since the Qur'an prohibits Muslims from breaking into sects (30:31-32), shouldn't we try to strengthen the Muslim *ummah* (community) on the basis of the Qur'an rather than divide ourselves on the basis of historical developments within the community? Shouldn't leaders of sects, who spew hatred against others, be found guilty of crimes committed by their followers?

12. Since the Qur'an emphasizes that God sent prophets* to all the nations of the world (Qur'an 10:47), that the Message has always been the same (Serve God and shun evil, Qur'an 16:36), and that

Muslims are to make no distinction among any of God's messengers* (Qur'an 4:152), shouldn't Muslims stop denigrating the beliefs and practices of others and see the same God in the house of worship of other religions? Since hating others has not worked so far, shall we not give loving others a chance?

13. Since the Qur'an declares that Muhammad* was no more than a messenger and that there were many other messengers* before him (Qur'an 3:144), should we deify the prophet and deal harshly with anyone who appears to "belittle" Muhammad* in any way? For example, I understand that some Pakistani scholar was imprisoned recently for asking whether Muhammad* was circumcised.

What percentage of Muslims, do you feel, may be violating the Qur'an, according to the examples you have given above?
Fortunately, the number may be small. The majority of Muslims, similar to the followers of other religions, are so much involved in trying to lead an honest God-fearing life that they generally don't have time to meddle into the affairs of others. However, as in most other societies, zealots often take on leadership roles. And because such individuals are committed to their cause and are usually intolerant and dogmatic, many self-respecting people keep their views to themselves rather than challenging these zealots.

How much support do such zealots enjoy in the Muslim community?
As far as I know, not too much. Often, the success of fundamental Muslim religious parties at local and national elections in several Muslim countries has been dismal. And, if they've won in the past because of some prevailing political condition (as in Iran after the downfall of the Shah), they've often lost it within a few years. Such zealots can only use force to gain or retain power; they are also highly intolerant of others who do not share their views.

What needs to be done to counter this situation?
The "silent majority" of Muslims–indeed of humanity–needs to unite
and speak out, peacefully. We should learn from such modern-day
"Sufis" as the late Rev. Martin Luther King, Jr., who said: "Violence
as a way of achieving justice is both impractical and immoral. It is
impractical because it is a descending spiral ending in destruction for
all. The old law of an eye for an eye leaves everybody blind. It is
immoral because it seeks to humiliate the opponent rather than to
convert. Violence is immoral because it thrives on hatred rather than
love. It destroys community and makes brotherhood impossible. It
leaves society in a monologue rather than dialogue. Violence ends by
defeating itself. It creates bitterness in the survivors and brutality in the
destroyers."

A thought-provoking article by Pervez Hoodbhoy bemoaning how
Muslims have slid from their glorious past to their current abyss
appeared in the daily Dawn, Karachi on December 10 and 11, 2001. It
can be accessed at http://www.dawn.com/2001/12/10/op.htm and
http://www.dawn.com/2001/12/11/op.htm.

What can the "silent majority" do?
On the following pages I offer a proposal for uniting people. Unlike
wars fought 1,400 years ago when an aggressor's sword would kill
only one person at a time, the current equivalent of that "aggressor's
sword"–nuclear weapons not to mention bio-terrorism and chemical
terrorism–can destroy millions. The stakes are far too high; the call of
zealots to hatred and intolerance should not go unchallenged:

> Hadeeth: The prophet said: "If anyone spends the night
> with grease on his hand, unwashed, he can blame only
> himself for any trouble caused" (Abu Dawood 3843).

Collectively, let us wash away that grease from all our hands.

CHAPTER 15. PROSPECTIVE SYNTHESIS:
"BELIEVERS ALL NETWORK"

Let all peace-loving people around the world proclaim, loudly and clearly, that we are all creatures of the same Ultimate Reality, a Reality which, while being called by different names in different religions, has always conveyed the same message of righteousness, peace, and love through all His prophets. Thus, rather than creating divisions among ourselves on the basis of our respective messengers, let us unite on the basis of the Message they all brought.

And while we may all have a "favorite" prophet, let us recognize and respect equally all prophets as messengers of the same God. Each prophet had something unique to offer. For example, from Abraham* we learn of the One Almighty God; from Moses*, the Ten Commandments; from Jesus*, the message of love and forgiveness; from Buddha*, the message of perfect meditation; from Lao Zi*, the message of living in harmony with nature; from the unnamed founder(s)* of Hinduism, the message of the multiple manifestations of the One Reality; from Mahavira*, the pathway for the perfection and purification of the soul; from Zoroaster*, the Spiritual Light of God; and from Muhammad*, an affirmation of the universality of God's Message. Therefore, let us not get bogged down by narrow-minded rules which divide us, but embrace the underlying broad principles which unite us. We cannot undo injustices of the past in the name of religion; but we help prevent these in the future.

Imagine how much more we could enrich ourselves if we assimilate the guidance of all these messengers and make their respective paths converge and become a part of our individual "super highway," with all of our respective "personal truths" converging in the direction of the "Ultimate Truth." Let us feel equally comfortable in praying to

Almighty Creator in the houses of worship of all religions. After all, God has affirmed that His name is commemorated in monasteries, churches, synagogues, and mosques (Qur'an 22:40). And while we may have differing rituals to help us reach that Reality, let us look beyond these and recognize the same Supreme Being everywhere.

Let us proclaim unequivocally that all humans are equal, with all of us having the same opportunity to reach Him, based only on our degree of righteousness. Let us remember that in our quest to reach that Ultimate Goal, we are not competing with each other, but only with our own egos, biases, and actions. Let us all move to the middle of the inner wheel of our respective religions, where the message of Truth and righteousness includes all colors of the Rainbow; a wheel which, when spun, produces that Big White Light. Let us affirm the following:

1. Our belief in God (by whatever name He may be called), His angels, all His messengers, His books, and the Day of Judgment.
2. Our belief that all humans are equal before God and that belief without righteous actions is insufficient in God's sight.
3. Our intention to respect equally all prophets of God, understand their respective messages, and enrich our lives accordingly. We will try to discover the common thread which runs through all prophetic messages. We also will respect religious reformers who have come in more recent times to help guide humanity back onto God's true path, from which we may have become "de-railed" by our own arrogance, ignorance, or closed mindedness.
4. Our intention to keep an open mind always, visit house of worship of all religions, and try to feel His presence everywhere.
5. Our desire to strive to spread the message of God through wisdom and beautiful preaching, to discuss religious issues with others in ways that are full of understanding and love, and to not get angry with those who may disagree with us.

Visit us at: http://www.believersall.net

CHAPTER 16. SUMMARY:
What Did We Learn About Islam?
Where do we go from here?

I hope, dear reader, you'll agree that Islam is different from what the actions of some Muslims might lead us to believe. Here is a chapter-wise summary of what we learned, along with some suggested Ijtihad.

PART A: THE CURRENT SITUATION

Chapter 1: Setting the Stage: Islam (submission to God) is a monotheistic faith based on belief in one Omnipotent, Omnipresent, and Omniscient God, who has existed forever and will be forever. He has neither ascendants nor descendants. Besides belief in God, Islam requires belief in God's angels, His prophets, His Books, and the Day of Judgment. Worshiping God is incomplete without righteous actions such as honesty, hard work, discipline, tolerance, and modesty. Rituals and practices without good work are considered empty.

Muslims use two information sources for religious guidance: (1) The Qur'an, which was revealed to Muhammad* by the archangel Gabriel over a 23-year period. (2) Hadeeth/Sunnah/Shariah, the purported sayings and actions of Muhammad*, compiled some 250-300 years after he had passed away and was no longer available to confirm the statement and actions being attributed to him. The strengths and shortcomings of various Hadeeth are discussed in Chapter 3.

With Muhammad's* death, Islamic history–development of the religion's concepts and beliefs–came to an end, and Muslim history–a record of human actions–began. These also led to the division of Muslims into Shias and Sunnis. This occurred because of disagreement over who should have succeeded Muhammad* as Khalifa (Caliph), the spiritual and temporal head of the Muslim community.

Chapter 2: The Qur'an and Science: Fourteen hundred years ago, the Qur'an asserted: (1) the "heavens and earth were all joined together before God split them apart"; (2) the universe is continuing to expand; (3) the universe will start contracting some time in the future and re-coalesce into a single mass; (4) God will then "recreate the creation"; (5) "all heavenly bodies are swimming along in fixed orbits"; (6) it took God six ayam to create the universe, with each yaum (singular of ayam) being "a long time period, such as 50,000 years of human reckoning"; (7) the earth was molded into its current shape in four ayam; (8) life evolved from water; (9) all living things were created in pairs; (10) the human embryo develops "in three veils of darkness"; and (11) humans will one day fly into space. How could an unlettered goatherd have arrived at these conclusions? Only through Divine inspiration.

Chapter 3: Hadeeth: Strengths and Shortcomings: This chapter discusses some inherent shortcomings in the manner in which Hadeeth were collected and edited. It also cites examples of some Hadeeth which not only contradict one another but, in some cases, also appear to contradict the Qur'an. However, Hadeeth still have great value and are used throughout this book. They must always be used with care, with the Qur'an serving as the ultimate touchstone for their validity.

☞Ijtihad: Shouldn't Muslims engage in serious and objective dialogue to determine which Hadeeth should be followed and which ignored? This dialogue has to start with a realization that, unlike the sacred Qur'an, Hadeeth are a collection of anecdotal accounts of the prophet's* sayings and actions, compiled by humans some 250-300 years after he* died and was not available to confirm them.

☞Ijtihad: Shouldn't Muslims who follow Hadeeth dogmatically also drink camel's urine for its therapeutic value (Bukhari 1.234)? And shouldn't such Muslim men also have, as their first wife, some divorced woman who is 18-20 years older than them?

☞Ijtihad: Which has higher authority: the Qur'an or Hadeeth?

☞Ijtihad: Finally, let me reiterate the following Hadeeth:

> Hadeeth: Whoever revives a Sunnah which dies after me will be rewarded in the Hereafter; and whoever introduces some evil innovation which was not approved by God or His messenger, will be punished (Tirmidhi 168),

and remind my readers that I am not suggesting any innovations in Hadeeth; I am only suggesting that we should perhaps ignore those Hadeeth which seem to be innovations and contradict the Qur'an.

Chapter 4: The Islamic Belief System and Universality of God's Message: This chapter summarizes the five Muslim articles of faith: Belief in One God, His angels, His prophets, His Books, and the Day of Judgment. We are also reminded of the Qur'an's unequivocal assertion that God has sent prophets to all the nations of the world and that Muslims are to respect them all equally–not only the 24 prophets named in the Book.

☞Ijtihad Who could be among God's unnamed prophets? Since they all must have preached the same message of belief in One God and enjoined humans to lead a righteous life, shouldn't we include the founders of Buddhism (Gautama Siddhartha*), Confucianism (Confucius*), Daoism (Lao Zi*), Jainism (Vardhamana Mahavira*), Zoroastrianism (Zoroaster*), and the unnamed founder of Hinduism* in this group? They all preached about that Unseen Power and asked humans to lead righteous lives (although the message may have been misinterpreted by followers in some cases). What about sages of other peoples around the world? What about Ikhnaton, the Egyptian pharaoh who preached monotheism?

☞Ijtihad How do we define a Muslim? Shouldn't anyone who believes in One God, respects all God's prophets, and leads a righteous life be considered a Muslim?

Chapter 5: Muslim Rituals and Actions: This chapter lists many righteous actions such as honesty, discipline, hard work, and tolerance that Muslims are <u>required</u> to engage in, as well as many "unrighteous" actions such as stealing, arrogance, bigotry, and intolerance that we <u>required</u> to keep away from. Also summarized are the so-called "Five Pillars of Islam:" belief, prayers, fasting, pilgrimage, and charity. However, the chapter laments, the over-emphasis on these "pillars" in some Muslim societies has unfortunately resulted in these being projected as the <u>only</u> things needed to be a good Muslim. Thus, all other righteous duties get "second billing."

☛Ijtihad Isn't this overemphasis on the "five pillars" misplaced, especially since the Qur'an does <u>not</u> categorize these activities as "pillars of Islam" anywhere? Does God need our prayers and fasting? Doesn't He command us to pray, observe the fast, and go on pilgrimage to help us become better humans, "for prayer restrains from shameful and unjust deeds" (Qur'an 29:45)? Thus, shouldn't these rituals be considered as the means to help us become better humans–rather than being considered as ends in themselves?

☛Ijtihad If these rituals are considered "Pillars of Islam," shouldn't other righteous deeds (including charity) be called the "Foundation of Islam," without which empty rituals will be meaningless?

Chapter 6: Violence and Jihad: Jihad actually means "to strive for righteousness"; to do good for humanity; and to develop ourselves spiritually. These enjoy a much higher status in the eyes of God than armed struggle–which itself is permitted <u>only</u> in defense when attacked by an enemy who wants to drive Muslims out of their homes and deprive them of their means of livelihood <u>because of their religion</u>. A purely political war would not be called a jihad. And violence is to cease once the enemy is defeated. The innocent are to be protected.

While undoubtedly some Muslims spread Islam by the sword, in many cases conversion was also brought about by peaceful missionary work.

For example, no Muslim army has ever set foot in Indonesia, the world's most populous Muslim country; or in China, Russia, and other southeast Asian countries, where sizable Muslim populations exist. We also learn that pagan Mongols, who conquered Baghdad and other Muslim countries, converted to Islam–the religion of the people they conquered..

The "hatred" against America expressed by some Muslims is not on religious grounds, but because of what they consider as America's lopsided policy in the Middle East. Palestinians cite the numerous resolutions passed by the United Nations condemning Israel for its unjust policies in the Occupied Territories as vindicating their struggle. In many of these resolutions, the only country siding with Israel has been the U.S.

Finally, the September 11th tragedy cannot be defended by any passage in the Qur'an or Hadeeth. While many analysts suggest that this tragedy was triggered by, what they consider to be, America's lopsided in the Middle East, taking innocent lives anywhere cannot be condoned; nor can it help solve political problems in modern times.

☛Ijtihad: How do we deal with the disproportionate loss of Afghan lives in America's "war on terrorism" and Palestinian lives at the hand of Israelis?

☛Ijtihad: Who should be authorized to issue a call for "holy war?" What should be the pre-conditions for such a call? Against whom could such a war be directed? How do we prevent individuals with their own hidden agenda from issuing such a call? How do we protect the innocent in such an event?

☛Ijtihad Since God requires Muslims to "Invite (all) to the Way of your Lord with wisdom and beautiful preaching; and discuss with them in ways that are best and most gracious" (Qur'an 16:125), shouldn't Muslims spread Islam by interacting with followers of other religions in a peaceful way and participating in community activities rather than by adopting a "hostile" and "holier than thou" approach?

☛Ijtihad: Since God has declared: "Let there be no compulsion in religion" (Qur'an 2:256), shouldn't non-Muslims living in Muslim countries be free to practice their own religion–and also to engage in missionary activities? After all, Muslims have freedom to practice their religion and engage in missionary activities in non-Muslim countries.

☛Ijtihad: Wouldn't getting Americans sympathetic to the Palestinian cause elected to the U.S. Congress be a positive, peaceful, and longer-lasting way of getting a just solution to the Israel-Palestinian problem?

Chapter 7: Status of Women and Effeminate Men: The Qur'an accords equal rights to both men and women. It requires both to be modestly dressed, with women asked to cover their bosoms and wear an outer garment in public. There is no description of what constitutes an "outer garment." The only "dress code" mentioned in the Qur'an pertained only to Muhammad's* wives, and only when people visited his house: in such cases, visitors were to speak to his wives from "before a screen" (*hijab*). We may call this a "behavioral code," not a "dress code." Even the prophet's wives had only to wear an outer garment "when abroad"–and were not confined by "*hijab*"on such occasions. There is no criticism of eunuchs and effeminate men in the Qur'an.

☛Ijtihad: Since the Qur'anic instruction for hijab was issued only for men visiting the prophet's house, and only when they spoke to his wives, why should we apply this guideline for how Muslim women should be dressed in today's society?

☛Ijtihad: What constitutes "modest dress" for men and women? What is a suitable "outer garment" for women to "cover their bosoms?" Is a Muslim woman wearing skirt and blouse any less "Islamic" than a completely veiled woman? Shouldn't we let women decide what constitutes "modest dress" in their respective cultures?

Chapter 8: Marriage, Divorce, Inheritance. And Circumcision:
(a) <u>Marriage</u>: Having up to four wives is permitted to provide protection and support to widows, divorcees, and orphans girls–and that too only if the husband can treat all wives equally. (b) <u>Divorce</u>: A man can divorce his wife by saying "I divorce you" three times–but each pronouncement is to be separated by a menstrual cycle (iddah) to ensure there is no pregnancy and to provide an opportunity for reconciliation. During iddah, women are to live in the same style as previously. Maintenance is to be provided to former wives. Women can also initiate divorce proceedings against their husbands. (c) <u>Inheritance</u>: People must prepare their wills before death; they could even give all their property to daughters. When there is no will, the Qur'an provides a formula for property division. (d) <u>Circumcision</u>: There is no mention of this in the Qur'an; and Hadeeth present conflicting reports.

☞Ijtihad: Since only one of Muhammad's* wives was previously unmarried with the others being divorcees or widows, shouldn't devout Muslims, who base their lives on Hadeeth, follow the same approach, with the first wife even being older than them?

☞Ijtihad: Shouldn't the cruel treatment meted out to wives in some Muslim societies be declared illegal and un-Islamic, with abusive husbands being subject to appropriate punishment?

Chapter 9: Adultery: (1) Punishment for adultery (whether involving married or unmarried people) in the Qur'an is 100 stripes, with the guilty being permitted to marry other "equally guilty" person after their punishment. (2) A person is guilty of adultery only by: (a) confession; (b) having four adult witnesses to the actual act, but without forcible entry into the room or peeping for the purpose; or (c) pregnancy, but without rape. (3) The wife's oath that she is innocent of adultery charges is superior to her husband's oath accusing her of adultery.

☞Ijtihad: Should people be stoned beheaded for adultery when the Qur'an prescribes 100 lashes and permits them to marry other "similarly guilty" person after receiving their punishment?

☞Ijtihad: Since the guilty are to survive this punishment and are permitted to marry other "similarly guilty" persons thereafter, (1) isn't the psychology of punishment more important than its physical severity? And (2) couldn't the guilty couple marry each other after receiving their punishment?

Chapter 10: Food, Drink, Gambling, and Usury: (1) Eating pork is prohibited; but even this is permitted out of necessity. (2) Any meat can be eaten by reciting "Bismillah" ("I begin in the name of God") before eating. (3) Muslims are advised to refrain from drinking intoxicants, offering prayers with "befogged minds," and gambling. (4) Muslims are forbidden from practicing *riba*, which the Qur'an describes as the "doubling and redoubling" of money. This is interpreted as prohibition against charging or accepting guaranteed interest. Neither the Qur'an nor Hadeeth define what constitutes *riba*.

☞Ijtihad: If meat becomes edible by reciting Bismillah, is insistence on halal meat (meat slaughtered in a certain way) necessary?

☞Ijtihad: Isn't the Qur'anic advice vis-a-vis intoxicants actually a prohibition against getting drunk rather than against drinking?

☞Ijtihad: What should be the "cut-off period" for money being "doubled and redoubled" and labeled as *riba*? Is it *riba*, for example, if the money doubles in a week? a month? a year? in 10 years? in 20 years? At a 5% annual compounded growth rate, money will double in about 15 years. Is this *riba*? (2) How does one cope with inflation in long-term loans if the creditor is not permitted protection against the decreasing value of money over time through inflation?

Chapter 11: Slaves and Orphans: Even in the Middle Eastern society of 1,400 years ago, the Qur'an encouraged Muslims not only to treat slaves kindly, but also to set them free. Men were encouraged to marry female slave; and women, their male slave. Guardians are to discharge honestly their fiduciary responsibilities of managing the property of orphans.

Chapter 12: Amusement: Music, Dance, and Culture: (1) The Qur'an advises Muslims not to make religion difficult by putting obstacles in people's paths. It also clarifies that anything which is not specifically prohibited in the Book is acceptable. (2) There is no prohibition against entertainment, be it music, singing, dance, or poetry. These, of course, need to be in "good taste." (3) The prophet* appreciated and recited poetry, had music at his wedding, watched with his wife Aisha as Muslim women did some folk dance, and even organized a horse race.

☞Ijtihad: What forms of entertainment are not acceptable in Islam?

Chapter 13: Punishment for Crimes in this Life; Reward and Punishment in the Hereafter: The Qur'an declares that, while one is entitled to an "eye for an eye" in retaliatory punishment, it is better to forgive. We all will be accountable for our deeds in the Hereafter. No one can intercede on our behalf. The Qur'an asserts: The most honored of you in the sight of God is (the one who is) the most righteous.

PART B. WHERE DO WE GO FROM HERE?

Chapter 14: Introspective Analysis: In some cases, Muslim practices are at variance with Islamic teachings. Why? Since the Qur'an was revealed to Muhammad* over a period of 23 years, some Hadeeth might possibly pre-date Qur'anic injunctions on specific issues. Prior to receiving Divine guidance, the prophet may have, in some cases, followed Biblical injunctions. Nowadays, while Jews and Christians are not following some questionable Biblical injunctions, Muslims are, via some Hadeeth–disregarding the fact that Qur'anic injunctions might be different.

Chapter 15. Prospective Synthesis: Based on Qur'anic injunctions, this future-looking chapter underscores that we all are creatures of the same God and that, while our respective messengers may have been different, the Message has always been the same: Believe in One Almighty God (called by different names in different religions) and the lead a righteous life. The fact that all of us should respect all God's prophets (including those unnamed) is emphasized in no uncertain terms in the Qur'an (for example: "God will reward those who believe in God and His messengers and make no distinction among any of these messengers" (Qur'an 4:152).

☛ Ijtihad: Shouldn't all those who believe in One Almighty God unite in a network (<u>Believers All Network</u>) and strive to bring about unity, equality, tolerance, and justice for all, and in this way enhance the quality of life on the planet which we all share?

Chapter 16: Book Summary: This final chapter distills information from the previous chapters and reiterates that a <u>Believers all Network</u> be formed. Comments are invited from our readers to help make this Network effective. Readers are also requested to visit our website: <u>http://www.believersall.net</u>.

May peace be with you!

APPENDIX. ATTRIBUTES OF GOD
MENTIONED IN THE QUR'AN
(Based on Tirmidhi 2285)

[Note: The English equivalents of these Arabic terms should be taken as approximate only. Different translators have used somewhat different equivalents].

English	Arabic	English	Arabic
Abaser	*Al-Khafid*	Everlasting	*Al-Baaqi*
Able	*Al-Qaadir*	Evolver	*Al-Bari*
Alive	*Al-Hayy*	Exalted, Most	*Al-Muta'ali*
All-Embracing	*Al-Wasi'*	Exalter	*Ar-Rafi*
All-Forgiving	*Al-Ghafoor*	Expander	*Al-Basit*
All-Hearing	*As-Samee*	Expediter	*Al-Muqaddim*
All-Knowing	*Al-Alim*	Faith,	*Al-Mumin*
All-Seeing	*Al-Baseer*	Guardian of	
Appreciative	*Ash-Shakoor*	Fashioner	*Al-Musawwir*
Avenger	*Al-Muntaqim*	Finder	*Al-Waajid*
Aware	*Al-Khabeer*	Firm One	*Al-Mateen*
Beneficent	*Ar-Rahman*	First, The	*Al-Awwal*
Bestower	*Al-Wahhaab*	Forbearing One	*Al-Haleem*
Compassionate	*Ar-Ra'oof*	Forgiver	*Al-Ghaffar*
Compeller	*Al-Jabbar*	Gatherer	*Al-Jame'*
Constrictor	*Al-Qabid*	Generous One	*Al-Kareem*
Creator	*Al-Khaliq*	Glorious, Most	*Al-Majeed*
Death,		Goodness,	
Creator of	*Al-Mumeet*	Source of	*Al-Barr*
Delayer	*Al-Mu'akhkhir*	Governor	*Al-Wali*
Dishonerer	*Al-Muzill*	Great, Most	*Al-Kabeer*
Distresser	*Ad-Darr*	Great One	*Al-Azim*
Enricher	*Al-Mughni*	Guide	*Al-Haadi*
Equitable	*Al-Muqsit*	Guide to the	
Eternal	*As-Samad*	Right Path	*Ar-Rasheed*

Hidden	*Al-Batin*	Praiseworthy	*Al-Hameed*
High, Most	*Al-'Ali*	Preserver	*Al-Hafeez*
Holy	*Al-Quddus*	Preventer	*Al-Maani'*
Honorer	*Al-Mu'izz*	Propitious	*An-Nafi'*
Incomparable	*Al-Baadi'*	Protecting	
Inheritor	*Al-Waarith*	Friend	*Al-Wali*
Judge	*Al-Hakkam*	Protector	*Al-Muhaymin*
Just	*Al-'Adl*	Provider	*Ar-Razzaaq*
Last	*Al-Akhir*	Reckoner	*Al-Haseeb*
Life, Giver of	*Al-Muhyi*	Reckoner	*Al-Muhsi*
Light	*An-Noor*	Repentance,	*At-Tawwab*
Loving	*Al-Wadood*	Acceptor of	
Maintainer	*Al-Miqeet*	Responsive	*Al-Mujeeb*
Majesty and	*Dhul-Jalaal-*	Restorer	*Al-Mu'eed*
Splendor,	*Wal-Ikram*	Resurrector	*Al-Ba'ith*
Lord of		Self-Subsisting	*Al-Qayuum*
Majestic	*Al-Mutakabbir*	Self-Sufficient	*Al-Ghani*
Manifest	*Az-Zahir*	Sovereign Lord	*Al-Malik*
Merciful	*Ar-Rahim*	Sovereignty,	
Mighty	*Al-Aziz*	Owner of	*Malik-ul-Mulk*
Most Great	*Al-Kabeer*	Strong, Most	*Al-Qawi*
Noble, The	*Al-Maajid*	Subduer	*Al-Qahhar*
One, The	*Al-Ahad*	Sublime One	*Al-Jaleel*
Opener	*Al-Fattah*	Subtle One	*Al-Lateef*
Originator,	*Al-Mubdi*	Trustee	*Al-Wakeel*
Pardoner	*Al-'Afuw*	Truth, The	*Al-Haqq*
Patient	*As-Saboor*	Unique	*Al-Waahid*
Peace,	*As-Salaam*	Watchful	*Ar-Raqeeb*
Source of		Wise	*Al-Hakeem*
Powerful	*Al-Muqtadir*	Witness	*As-Shahid*

REFERENCES

Alim, The (CD). Islamic Software Corporation (1986).

Akins, James (2000). The Attack on the *USS Liberty* and its Cover-up. The Center for Policy Research on Palestine., Washington, DC. http://www.palestinecenter.org.

Ali, Yusuf. (1989). The Holy Qur'an. Amana Corp. Brentwood, MD.

American Educational Trust. Washington Report on Middle East Affairs. Published nine times a year. http://www.wrema.org.

Asad, Mohammad (1980): The Message of the Qur'an. Dar al-Andalus Limited, 3 Library Ramp, Gibraltar.

Ateek, Naim Stifan (1989). Justice Ad Only Justice: A Palestinian Theology of Liberation. Orbis Books, Maryknoll, NY 10545.

Avnery, Uri (1968). Israel Without Zionism: a Plea for Peace in the Middle East. The MacMillan Company.

Azami, Mustafa (1978). Studies in Hadith Methodology and Literature. American Trust Publishing Company, Indiana.

Bucaille, M. (1976). The Bible, the Qur'an, and Science. The Crescent Publishing Co., 4 Abdul Qadir Market, Aligarh, India.

Bukkyo Dendo Kyokai (1997). The Teachings of Buddha*. Tokyo, Japan 108. Phone: (03) 3455-5851.

Chomsky, Naom (1999). Fateful Triangle: The United States, Israel, and Palestine. Southend Press.

Dougan Publishers, Inc. (1985).   The Holy Bible, in King James version. Gordonsville, TN.

Findley, P. (1991). They Dare to Speak Out: People and Institutions Confront Israeli Lobby. Chicago Press Review, Inc.

Grose, Peter. (1982). "The Partition Plan of Palestine 35 Years Ago." The New York Times Magazine, November 21

Herzl, Theodor (1989). The Jewish State. Dover Publishing, Inc.

Hoodbhoy, Pervez (2001). "Muslims and the West." Dawn, Karachi. (December 10 and 11, 2001). http://dawn.com/2001/12/10/op.htm.

Ishaq, Ibn (died 150 A.H.). Sirat Rasul Allah. I consulted its English translation by A. Guillaume (1979). The Life of Muhammad. Oxford University Press, Karachi.

Jewish Publication Society (1985). Tanakh, a new translation of the Holy Scriptures, Philadelphia.

Mahmood, S. Bashiruddin (1991). Qur'an and Science: Doomsday and Life after Death. Taha Publishers, Ltd., London (second edition).

Mernissi, Fatima (1991). The Veil and the Male Elite. Addison-Wesley Publishing Company (English translation).

Odeh, B.J. (1985). Lebanon: Dynamics of Conflict. Zed Press, London

Pravabhananda, S. and Manchester, F. (1957). The Upanishads. Mentor, Penguin Books.

Rahman, Fazlur. (1966). Islam. University of Chicago Press.

Said, Edward. (ed.) 1996. Covering Islam: How the Media and the Experts Determine How We See the Rest of the World. Random House.

Salibi, Kamal (1985). The Bible Came From Arabia. Jonathan Cape, London, England.

INDEX

(Underlined topics/numbers indicate pages on which some Biblical (B)
and Qur'anic (Q) passages dealing with violence, sexism,
death, inheritance, food, etc. are reproduced)

ABOUT THE AUTHOR

Saleem Ahmed was born in India (1939), raised in Pakistan, and now lives in Hawaii. He considers all three his home. He earned his M.S. degree in Geology at the University of Karachi in 1961 and his doctorate in Soil Science from the University of Hawaii in 1965, on a scholarship awarded by the East-West Center. The other "degree" he obtained in Hawaii was his wife, the former Carol Matsumoto, nicknamed Yasmin (after her Japanese name, Yasuko). Returning to Pakistan in 1965 with Yasmin, Saleem first taught soil science at the University of Karachi, then spent the next eight years with the Esso Pakistan Fertilizer Co., Ltd., his last position as Technical Services Advisor. Saleem spent the next 22 years with the East-West Center, Honolulu, and led their Botanical Pest Control project. Currently he works as a financial consultant in Honolulu, Hawaii.

Saleem's diverse publications include: Scrabble⁽ᴿ⁾ Word-Building Book, co-authored with his wife and both daughters (Pocket Books, Simon & Schuster, 1991); Handbook of Plants with Pest-Control Properties, co-authored with Michael Grainge (John Wiley & Sons, New York, 1988); and Agriculture-Fertilizer Interface in Asia: Issues of Growth and Sustainability (Oxford & IBH Publishers, New Delhi, 1995). He has contributed chapters to several professional publications, including the National Research Council's book NEEM: A Tree for Solving Global Problems (National Academy Press, Washington, DC, 1992).

Saleem teaches courses on Islam and Financial Planning at the University of Hawaii and elsewhere in the community. His multicultural outlook inspired him to conceive of *Milun*: Association for Promoting South Asian Culture, and the *One-Talk Club*, both of which are active community groups in Hawaii. As a "poet-in-training," Saleem wrote the lyrics to the song *Dhoond raha hoon* (which in Urdu and Hindi means "I am searching"), included in the CD *Dil-e-Ruba* produced by Blue Rains, a Honolulu-based music production group. Very much a "people person" Saleem enjoys learning about others and trying to see the world from their perceptions of reality.

BEYOND VEIL AND HOLY WAR:
Islamic Teachings and Muslim Practices with Biblical Comparisons

By Saleem Ahmed, Ph.D.
ISBN 0-9717655-0-2, 224 Pages, 6 x 9" Hardbound, $28.95

Go beyond the stereotypes for understanding and communication in the area of important world events. This book answers many searching questions non-Muslims are asking about this religion followed by one-fifth of humanity. Answers will surprise not only non-Muslims but also many Muslims as this book differentiates between what Islam preaches and what some Muslims practice.

Order your own copy today. Cost is **$28.95** plus **$4 US Priority Mail**, for a **total of $32.95.** Send check, money order, or Visa, MasterCard information to:

Moving Pen Publishers, Inc.
P.O. Box 25155, Honolulu, HI 96825

Name: _____

Address: _____

_____

Visa/Master Card No. _____

Expiration date on card _____

Name on the card (Please print) : _____

Signature of cardholder: _____

Anyone may make copies of this page for others to order the book. Please write the publisher about bulk and resale orders.